# T

# Life

# Beyond

# Death

By
Yogi Ramacharaka
(Willam Walker Atkinson)

Life Transformation Publishing

ISBN-13: 978-1723284007

ISBN-10: 1723284009

Life Transformation Publishing
All Rights Reserved 2018

# Contents

Chapters

I                    5
The Other Side
II                   9
There is NO Death
III                  13
The Planes Of Life
IV                   17
The Astral Plane
V                    21
After Death
VI                   25
The Soul-Slumber
VII                  29
The Soul's Awakening
VIII                 33
Astral Plane Geography
IX                   37
Primitive Soul State
X                    41
Astral Religious Experience
XI                   45
Astral Heavens and Hells
XII                  50
 Astral Self Expression
XIII                 56
 Astral Plane Occupation
XIV                  59
Astral Companionship
XV                   63
Spirit Communication
XVI                  67
Earth-Bound Souls
XVII                 71
Astral Shells

XVIII          75
The Second Soul-Sleep
XIX            79
Re-Birth
XX             83
Beyond Reincarnation

# CHAPTER I
## "THE OTHER SIDE"

One of the questions most frequently asked the teachers of the Wisdom of the East is this: "What do you teach regarding 'the other side' of the river of death'?" To the trained and developed occultist, this question never seems to lose its strangeness. To such, it would seem as the question: "What do you teach regarding the 'other side' of the street?" would seem to the ordinary man on the street. The latter would naturally feel surprised that there should be any question of "teaching" on the subject, for the inquirer would have but to use his own eyes to obtain the answer to his query.

The Oriental teacher never fails to wonder at the many evidences of the result of mere theory and dogmatic teaching on the part of the majority of the teachers and preachers of the Western world. These so-called teachers are like the "blind leading the blind," for they have no means of verifying their statements, and merely pass on what they have blindly received from others, who, in turn, have received their own instruction in the same way. In the Orient, on the contrary, one meets with so many persons of developed higher psychic and spiritual sense, to whom the phenomena of "the other side" is as familiar as is the phenomena of "this side," that the "other side" seems as real and actual as does the ordinary environment of earth-life. Among developed Orientals "the other side" is no uncharted sea, but has its currents, depths, islands, and general facts as clearly stated and understood as is the Atlantic Ocean by the Western mariner. Moreover, every educated Oriental is taught from youth that the phenomena of "the other side" need not be taken on faith, but may be actually known to those who will expend the time and study required for developing the higher senses which are possessed by all of the race.

But, from the same reasons, the developed Oriental occultist finds himself confronted with a most perplexing, not to say discouraging task when he attempts to convey his knowledge on this subject to Western students.

The Western mind instinctively refuses to accept truth in the manner of the mind of the Oriental student. Not having realized by actual experience certain fundamental psychic and spiritual facts, which serve as a basis for the detailed teaching, the Western mind naturally demands "actual proof "of these basic facts before being willing to proceed further. Inasmuch as these facts must first be experienced to be known, no amount of argument ever serves to bring that conviction of truth which should serve as the fundamental basis for the detailed teaching. Consequently by the Western student, the general basic statements of the teacher are accepted either purely on faith, or else regarded as mere guesses or speculation on the part of the teacher. And, as there are thousands of such guesses and speculative theories advanced in the Western world, the student may well be excused from refusing to accept any of them as truth, for, as he often argues, "one guess is as good as another." In the presentation of the facts of "the other side" to which the present volume is devoted, the student must realize from the beginning that there can be no actual physical proof afforded him, in the absence of a highly developed state of his higher psychic and spiritual senses. In his case, the proof demanded is akin to that asked of the blind man, who demands proof of scarlet or any other color of the article or like that asked by the deaf man, who demands proof of the existence of harmony in music. From the very nature of things, the proof cannot be afforded in such case. Imagine the attempt to explain the sensation of the taste of sugar to one who had never experienced the taste of anything sweet. How and where could one begin? How and where could one proceed?

So let us understand each other thoroughly, teacher, and students. Let us understand that the teachings of this book are not offered as proof of the phenomena of "the other side," but merely in the spirit of the traveller returned from some new and strange country, and who tells the tales of his journeying and the sights seen therein. As we said to the students of our first lessons, given to the Western world nine years ago: "We do not mean that the Eastern teachers insist upon the pupil blindly accepting every truth that is presented to him. On the contrary, they instruct the pupil to accept as truth only that which he can prove for himself, as no truth is truth to one until he can prove it by his own experiments. But the student is taught that before many truths may be so proven, he must develop and unfold. The teacher asks only that the student have confidence in him as a pointer-out of the way, and he says, in effect, to the student: "This is the way; enter upon it, and on the path you will find the things of which I have taught you; handle them, weigh them, measure them, taste them, and know for yourself. When you reach any point of the path you will know as much of it as did I or any other soul at that particular stage of the journey; but until you reach a particular point, you must either accept the statements of those who have gone before or reject the whole subject at that particular point. Accept nothing as final until you have proven it; but if you are wise, you will profit by the advice and experience of those who have gone before. Every man must learn by experience, but men may serve others as pointers of the way. At each stage of the journey it will be found that those who have progressed a little farther on the way, have left signs and marks and guide-posts for those who follow. The wise man will take advantage of these signs. I do not ask for blind faith, but only for confidence until you are able to demonstrate for yourselves the truths I am passing on to you, as they were passed on to me by those who went before"

The skeptical Western student may object that we offer no "scientific proofs" of the phenomena of "the other side." If by "scientific" he means the proofs of physical science, we agree with him. But to the advanced occultist, the term "scientific" has a much broader and wider meaning. The person who expects to weigh, measure and register spiritual things by physical standards has nothing but disappointment and failure before him, for he will never receive the proof he seeks. Physical apparatus is intended for physical objects only --- the world of spirit has its own set of apparatus, which alone is capable of registering its phenomena. Therefore we wish the matter clearly understood by the reader who is undertaking the study of this book. No physical proofs are offered. There are none such, strictly speaking, to be found anywhere. Moreover, there is no attempt at argument --- for there is no basis for argument between the seers of "the other side" and those whose vision is limited to the earth-plane.

But this does not mean that we are offering you a mass of irrational statements, and insisting that you take them on faith. Far from this is our intent. For while the reason alone can never hope to pierce the veil separating the two sides of Life-Death, nevertheless the reason, if allowed to follow its own reports divested of prejudice and blind adherence to teaching, will perceive a certain reasonableness in a true statement of the facts of the unknown --- it will seem that the teachings square with other accepted facts, and that they explain in a reasonable way phenomena otherwise unexplainable. In short, the reason will seem that the teachings of truth reconcile apparently opposing sets of facts, and join together many obscure bits of truth which one finds accepted by his reason, but which, heretofore, he has not been able to place together and join in a connected structure of mental concept.

The student is urged to suspend judgment until he has read carefully, and then as carefully considered, what we have to say. Then let him re-read, and re-consider the book as a whole. Then let him ask himself the honest question: "Does not this seem reasonable and probable." If he; can do no more than to accept it all as a "working hypotheses," by all means let him rest satisfied with that position --- although to us the term may evoke a smile when we realize that the teaching is built upon the experience and testimony of the wise of the ages. But, if the teaching is carefully read and considered, it will prove to be regarded as more and more reasonable as the years pass by with the individual. Fact after fact will be seen to fit into the general teaching, and, as older conceptions are discarded from time to time, these teachings will be found to take their place. It is not easy to escape from a truth, once it has been presented to you. It has a way of itching your mental ear, once it has lodged there. For behind that ear is a part of you, hidden though it may be, by many sheaths, which knows --- which KNOWS! Deny it though you may, you cannot escape from Truth once its seed has been lodged within your consciousness, for it will draw sustenance from your subconsciousness, and will in time sprout and put forth leaf and blossom.

So, after all, it matters little whether or not the student can fully grasp the teaching at this time. For Time is long, and one has all the time there is in which to master the lesson. All teachings, at the last, is but a process of seed-sowing.

# CHAPTER II

## "THERE IS NO DEATH"

The race has been hypnotized with the idea of Death. The common usage of the term reflects the illusion. We hear those who should know better speaking of persons being "cut down by the grim reaper;" "cut off in his prime," "his activities terminated;" "a busy life brought to an end;" etc., the idea expressed being that the individual had been wiped out of existence and reduced to nothingness. In the Western world this is particularly true. Although the dominant religion of the West teaches the joys of the "hereafter" in such strong terms that it would seem that every believer would welcome the transition; although it might well be supposed that relatives and friends would don gay robes and deck themselves with bright flowers in token of the passage of the loved one to a happier and brighter sphere of existence --- we see just the opposite manifestation. The average person, in spite of his faith and creed, seems to dread the approach of "the grim reaper," and his friends drape themselves in black robes and give every other outward token of having forever lost the beloved one. In spite of their beliefs, or expression of belief, Death has a terror which they seemingly cannot overcome.

To those who have acquired that sense of consciousness of the illusion of death, these frightful emotions have faded away. To them, while they naturally feel the sorrow of temporary separation and the loss of companionship, the loved one is seen to have simply passed on to another phase of life, and nothing has been lost --- nothing has perished. There is a centuries'-old Hindu fable, in which is told the tale of a caterpillar, who feeling the approach of the langour which betokened the end of the crawling stage of existence and the beginning of the long sleep of the chrysalis stage, called his friends around him. "It is sad," he said, "to think that I must abandon my life, filled with so many bright promises of future achievement. Cut off by the grim reaper, in my very prime, I am an example of the heartlessness of Nature. Farewell, good friends, farewell forever. Tomorrow I shall be no more." And, accompanied by the tears and lamentations of the friends surrounded his death-bed, he passed away. An old caterpillar remarked sadly: "Our brother has left us. His fate is also ours. One by one we shall be cut down by the scythe of the destroyer, like unto the grass of the field. By faith we hope to rise again, but perhaps this is but the voice inspired by a vain hope. None of us knows anything positively of another life. Let us mourn the common fate of our race." Whereupon, sadly, they departed.

9

The grim irony of this little fable is clearly perceived by all of us, and we smile at the thought of the ignorance which attended the first stage of the transformation of the lowly crawling thing into the glorious-hued creature, which in time will emerge from the sleep of death into a higher form of life. But, smile not, friends, at the illusion of the caterpillars --- they were but even as you and I. For the Hindu story-teller of centuries ago has pictured human ignorance and illusion in this little fable of the lower forms of life. All occultists recognize in the transformation stages of the caterpillar-chrysalis-butterfly a picture of the transformation which awaits every mortal man and woman. For death to the human being is no more a termination or cessation than is the death-sleep of the caterpillar. In neither case does life cease for even a single instant --- life persists while Nature works her changes. We advise every student to carry with him the lesson of this little fable, told centuries ago to the children of the Hindu race, and passed on by them from generation to generation.

Strictly speaking, from the Oriental point of view, there is no such thing as Death. The name is a lie --- the idea an illusion growing from ignorance. There is no death --- there is nothing but Life. Life has many phases and forms, and some of the phases are called "death" by ignorant men. Nothing really dies --- though everything experiences a change of form and activity. As Edwin Arnold so beautifully expresses it in his translation of the "Bhagavaad Gita":

"Never the spirit was born; The spirit shall cease to be never. Never was time it was not; End and beginning are dreams.

Birthless and deathless, and changeless, Remaineth the spirit forever Death hath not touched it at all, Dead though the house of it seems."

Materialists frequently urge as an argument against the persistence of life beyond the stage of death, the assumed fact that everything in nature suffers death, dissolution, and destruction. If such were really the fact, then indeed would it be reasonable to argue the death of the soul as a logical conclusion. But, in truth, nothing of this kind happens in nature. Nothing really dies. What is called death, even of the smallest and apparently most inanimate thing, is merely a change of form and condition of the energy and activities which constitute it. Even the body does not die, in the strict sense of the word. The body is not an entity, for it is merely an aggregation of cells, and these cells are merely material vehicles for a certain form of energy which

10

animates and vitalizes them. When the soul passes from the body, the units composing the body manifest repulsion for each other, in place of the attraction which formerly held them together.

The unifying force which has held them together withdraws its power, and the reverse activity is manifested. As a writer has well said: "The body is never more alive than when it is dead." As another writer has said: "Death is but an aspect of Life, and the destruction of one material form is but a prelude to the building up of another." So the argument of the materialist really lacks its major premise, and all reasoning based thereon must be faulty and leading to a false; conclusion.

But the advanced occultist, or other spiritually developed person, does not require to seriously consider the argument of the materialists, nor would he even though these arguments were a hundred times more logical. For such a person has awakened within himself the higher psychic and spiritual faculties whereby he may actually know that the soul perishes not when the body dissolves. When one is able to leave the physical body behind, and actually travel in the regions of "the 'other side," as in the case of many advanced individuals, any purely speculative discussions or arguments on the realty of "life after death" take on the appearance of absurdity and futility.

If an individual, who has not as yet reached the stage of psychical and spiritual discernment whereby he is given the evidence of the higher sense on the question of the survival of the soul, finds his reason demanding something akin to "proof," let him turn his mental gaze inward instead of outward, and there he will find that which he seeks. For, at the last, as all philosophy teaches us, the world of the inner is far more real than is the world of the outer phenomena. In fact, man has no actual knowledge of the outer --- all he has is the report of the inner upon the impressions received from the outer. Man sees not the tree at which he is gazing --- he perceives but the inverted image of that tree pictured upon his retina. Nay, more, his mind does not even see this image, for it receives only the vibratory report of the nerves whose ends have been excited by that image. So we need not be ashamed of taking mental stock of the inner recesses of our mind, for many of the deepest truths are recorded there.

In the great subconscious and super-conscious regions of the mind are to be found a knowledge of many fundamental truths of the universe. Between two of these truths most strongly impressed there are these (1) the certainty of the existence of a Supreme Universal Power, under, back of, and supporting the phenomenal world; (2) the certainty of the immortality of the Real Self --- that Something Within which fire cannot destroy, water cannot drown, nor air blow away. The mental eye turned inward will always find the "I," with the certainty of its imperishability.

It is true that this is a different kind of proof from that required regarding material and physical objects, but what of that? The truth sought is a fact of spiritual inner life, and not of the physical outer life --- therefore it must be looked for within, and not without, the soul itself. The objective intellect concerns physical objects alone --- the subjective intellect, or intuition, concerns psychical and spiritual objects; the one the body of things, the other the soul of things. Look for knowledge, concern either class of things in his own appropriate region of your being.

Let the soul speak for itself, and you will find that its song will ring forth clearly, strongly, and gloriously: "There is no Death; there is no Death; there is no Death; there is naught but Life, and that Life is LIFE EVERLASTING!" Such is the song of the soul. Listen for it is the Silence, for there alone can its vibrations reach your eager ears. It is the Song of Life ever denying Death. There is no Death --- there is naught but Life Everlasting, forever, and forever, and forever.

# CHAPTER III

## THE PLANES OF LIFE

One of the elementary ideas of the Yogi Philosophy most difficult for the ordinary Western mind to grasp and assimilate is that of the "planes" of life. This difficulty is most apparent when the Western student attempts to grasp the Yogi teachings regarding "the other side." The Western thought insists upon the concept of the realm of the life of the disembodied soul as a place, or places. The Western theology is responsible for this, to a great extent, although there is also to be considered the tendency of the Western mind to think in terms of objective existence, even when life apart from the objective is being considered. The average Western religionist insists upon thinking of "heaven" as a place situated somewhere in space, containing beautiful mansions of precious stones, situated on streets paved with gold. Even those who have outgrown this childish idea find it difficult to conceive of their heaven as a state rather than a place. The Western mind finds it hard to form the abstract concept, and naturally falls back on the old idea of a heaven in space.

The Oriental mind, on the contrary, finds it quite easy to grasp the idea of the several planes of existence. Centuries of familiar thought on the subject has rendered the concept as clear and definite as that of place. We have met Western thinkers who smilingly confessed that they could not divest their concept of "planes "with that of a level strata, or layer of some kind of material substance. But this conception is as far from the truth as is the idea of mere place. A plane is a state, not a place in any sense of the word. And the student must learn to eliminate the idea of place from that of plane.

A plane is a condition or state of activity in the eternal energy of spirit in which the Cosmos lives, and moves and has its being. In any given point of space there may be many planes of activity. Taking our examples from the physical world, let us use the ordinary vibration of sound as an illustration. The air may be filled with many notes of the musical scale. Each note is simply a certain degree of vibration of the air. The notes occupy the same position in space, and yet do not conflict with each other so far as space filling qualities are concerned. It is an axiom of physics that no two bodies of matter can occupy the same space at the same time. But thousands of these vibratory notes may occupy the same space at the same time. This is borne upon one when he listens to some great orchestral rendering a musical composition. Many instruments are playing at the same time, and the air is filled with countless vibrations, and yet one may pick out any particular instrument if he chooses, and even particular notes may be distinguished. No note is lost, and yet the entire volume is manifested in the small space of the ear drum. This is a somewhat rude illustration, but it may serve to accustom the mind to form the proper concept.

Another illustration, this time on a little higher scale, is that of the vibrations of light. Light, we know, appears as the result of the vibratory waves of the ether coming in contact with physical matter. Each color has its own place on the vibratory scale. Each ray of sunshine that reaches us is composed of a great variety of colors --- the colors of the spectrum, which may be separated by means of certain prismatic instruments. All of the colors are to be found in every point of space in which the ray of sunlight appears. They are all there, and may be separated and registered apart from the others. Moreover, beyond the realm of light visible to the human eye, there are many colors invisible to the human sight by reason of their vibrations being either too high or two low. These invisible colors may be detected by means of instruments. Perhaps these varying rates of color vibrations may help you to form the idea of the space less planes of existence.

Another illustration may be found in the field of electricity, in which we find fresh instances of various degrees and condition of energy occupying the same space at the same time. On improved telegraphic apparatus we find many messages passing in each direction along the same wire, each independent, and none interfering with the others. In the same way, the air may be filled with a thousand wireless-telegraphic messages, attuned to different keys and consequently not interfering with each other. The various vibrations interpenetrate each other, each seemingly being unaware of the presence of the other and not being affected by it. It is conceivable, even, that there might be a dozen worlds occupying the same portion of space, but each being keyed on a far different vibratory scale of matter, and yet none interfering with the other, the living things on each being totally unaware of the existence of those of the other. Scientific writers have amused themselves by writing fanciful stories of such a series of worlds, and indeed they wrote better than they knew, for they symbolized a metaphysical truth in physical terms.

But, it may be objected, does the Yogi Philosophy teach that these planes of Life are but varying forms of vibrations of matter? Not at all. Far from it. The teaching is that each plane represents a different degree of vibratory energy --- but not of matter. Matter is merely a very low form of vibratory energy --- even the finest form of matter. There are forms of matter as much higher than the finest of which the ordinary physical scientist has knowledge, as his finest matter is higher than the hardest rock. And beyond the plane of matter rise plane upon plane of super material energy, of which the mind of physical science does not even dare to dream. And yet, for the purpose of the illustration, we may say that it is possible to think of every one of the planes manifesting in the same point of space at the same time. So you see, the conception of planes has nothing whatever in common with that of space. In view of the foregoing, the student will see that when we speak of the planes of existence of "the other side," we are far from meaning to indicate places or regions of space. The Yogi Philosophy has naught to do with doctrines of heavens or hells or purgatories in the sense of places. It knows of no such places, or regions, although it recognizes the real basis of the teachings which hold to the same. In this particular volume, we shall not attempt to consider the general question of the countless planes of existence manifesting in the universe. The scope of this particular work confines us to the consideration and description of those particular planes of the Astral World which are concerned in the manifestation of the existence of the disembodied souls of the dwellers upon earth the so-called "spirit-world" of the human race. We shall see that there are many planes and sub-planes of existence on the great Astral Plane of Life --- generally known as The Astral World, in order to distinguish it from the Physical World below it in the vibratory scale. Each plane and sub-plane has its own distinguishing characteristics and phenomena, as we shall see as we proceed. And yet the same general laws, principles, and characteristic qualities are common to all.

Finally, before we pass on the consideration of the Astral Plane, let us once more endeavor to fix in your minds the proper conception of the real nature of that which we know as "planes." When we speak of "rising" from a lower to a higher plane, or of "descending" from a higher to a lower plane, we do not wish to be understood as picturing an ascent or decent of steps. Nor are we picturing a rising or descending from one layer or strata to another. Even the familiar symbol of rising from the ocean depths to its surface, is incorrect. The nearest mental picture possible to be made of the transition from plane to plane, is that of increase or decrease of vibrations as evidenced in sound-waves, light waves, or waves of electricity. By tightening a violin string, one may raise its degree of vibration and therefore its note. The same may be done by heating a bar of iron causing its color to change gradually

15

from a dull red to a delicate violet or white. Or in the case of a current of electricity, the power may be raised or lowered at will. If a still more material illustration be required, we have the case of the hardest mineral which may be changed into an invisible vapor simply by raising its degree of vibrations by heat. What is true on the lower planes of manifestation, is true of the higher. The transition from higher to lower, or lower to higher may be thought of (if desired) as a change of vibration in the energy of which all things are composed. This will come about as near to the truth as our imperfect powers of conception and comparison will permit. There are no words to express the higher phenomena --- all illustration in terms of the lower planes are crude, imperfect, and unsatisfactory. But even by these lowly symbols may the mind of man learn to grasp the ideas of things above the ordinary senses, and beyond the power of ordinary terms to express.

And, now, with the above firmly fixed in your minds, let us proceed to a consideration of the Great Astral Plane of Existence.

# CHAPTER IV

## THE ASTRAL PLANE

Students of occultism, Oriental and Occidental, find many references in the works of the old authorities, to that great series of planes, immediately above those of the material world, which are loosely styled the "Astral Plane." But they find the various authorities differing in their usage of the term. Many of the older authorities use the term, as we shall in this book, to designate the entire series of planes lying between those of the material world and those very exalted planes of existence, known as the "Spiritual Planes "the very nature of which is beyond the comprehension of the mind of the average man. On the other hand, some of the modern Western writers on the subject use the term the "Astral Plane "to indicate merely the lower planes and sub-planes of the Astral series --- those planes which blend into the material planes on the one hand and into the higher Astral planes on the other. This has caused some confusion in the minds of those beginning the study of the planes above the material.

In this book, as in our previous volumes, we follow the example of the ancient authorities, and apply the term, as they did, to the entire great series of planes lying between the material planes and the highest spiritual planes. We consider this plan preferable, for the reason that it is more simple, and tends to prevent the student from being confused by reason of many technical distinctions.

The Astral Plane is composed of numberless planes and sub-planes, and divisions of sub-planes, rising in a gradually ascending scale from those which touch and blend in with the higher material planes, to those which touch and blend into the lower strata (if the term may be so used) of the great spiritual planes. But between these two extremes is to be found the greatest possible variety of phenomena and phases of existence. On the lower planes of the Astral are manifested the psychic activities which men know as clairvoyance, clairaudience, telepathy, psychometry, etc. On other of the lower planes of the Astral are to be found certain forms of the "ghosts," "spooks," and other apparitions of disembodied souls which occasionally are perceived and sensed by man and some of the lower animals. On certain of these planes, also, the Astral bodies of men still in the flesh travel and manifest activity, either during the sleep of the owner of the body, or in certain trance conditions, or else when the owner deliberately leaves the physical body for the time being and projects his Astral Body on the Astral Plane.

The Astral colors are auras, which surround the physical bodies of all human beings, also manifest on certain sub-planes of the Astral. Certain other sub-planes may be called "the planes of psychic forces" by means of which various forms of psychic phenomena are performed. On similar lower planes are to be found the "thought-forms," "thought-waves," thought-clouds," etc., emanating from the minds of human beings, which travel about affecting the thoughts and emotions of those who attract them and who are attuned to their own psychic keynote. We mention these only in passing, and for general information, rather than in detail, for these phenomena have been considered in other volumes of these series of books.

Some of the lower sub-planes of the Astral are far from being healthy or agreeable places to visit, or upon which to function, for the untrained person. In fact the experienced occultist has as little to do with them as possible, and advise all dabblers in occultism to avoid these miasmatic psychic regions as he would a swampy, fever-laden region on the material plane. Many persons have wrought great injury to themselves from attempting to penetrate these lower planes without a correct knowledge of the nature thereof, many having wrecked their bodies and minds by foolishly producing or inducing psychic conditions which cause them to function on these lower psychic planes. The old adage which informs us "that fools rush in where angels fear to tread," applies in full force in this case.

Some of these lower Astral sub-planes are filled with Astral forms of disembodied human beings, the higher principles of whom are still attached to the Astral body, and which are held earth-bound by reason of the attraction of the material world. In this region also dwell for a time the very scum of disembodied human life, having every attraction to hold them down to the things of the material world, and nothing to draw them upward. It is pitiful to see persons, who would not think of associating with this class of persons in the flesh, nevertheless welcoming psychic intercourse and communication with the same class in the Astral, accepting them as "blessed spirits" and "beautiful souls." The disgust which comes to many persons who dapple in "spirit return" at a certain class of seances, is readily understood when we understand the character of the entities which inhabit these low planes. Some of these scoundrelly dwellers on the lower Astral planes frequently counterfeit friends and relations of the inquirer, much to the pained surprise of the latter.

As the planes ascend in degree we leave this class of entities behind, and enter the realms where abide the disembodied souls of those of higher degrees of spirituality. Higher and higher rise the scale of planes and sub-planes, until at last are reached the realms of the blessed --- the temporary abiding place of those who have attained a high degree of spiritual development, the "heaven worlds" which the religions of the race have sought to define according to their creeds and traditions. And, just as in the creeds of the race have been postulated the existence of "hells" to oppose the idea of "heaven," so in the Astral world, as might be expected, are to be found certain lower planes in which dwell the disembodied souls of persons of brutal natures and tendencies, in which the inevitable result of their earth-life is worked out. But these hells of the Astral are not eternal --- the disembodied soul in turn may work out into a better environment --- may be given "another chance." The Catholic conception of "purgatory" also has its Astral existence, in the form of certain sub-planes in which, as Hamlet's fathers ghost has said: "the foul crimes done in my days of nature are burned and purged away "--- but not in the fire of materiality, the fires of memory and imagination sufficing.

In short, on the great Astral plane are to be found conditions corresponding with nearly, if not all, of the conceptions formed by the mind of man in connection with the religions of all times and places. These conceptions have not arisen by mere chance --- they are the result of the experience of certain of the race who in some way established psychic connection with some of the many Astral Planes, each of whom, according to his own nature and inclinations, reported his experiences to his fellows, who afterward incorporated them in the various religions of the world. It will be remembered that every race of human beings has had its traditions of the "place" of departed souls, the description varying greatly and yet all agreeing in some particulars. As we proceed, we will see how these reports were obtained, and how the varying reports may be harmonized and understood in connection with each other.

The term "Astral" of course means "of or pertaining to the stars." It originally came into use in connection with occultism by reason of the common idea of men that "the other side" is "up in the skies;" among the clouds, or in the regions of the stars. Even in our own day, when the idea of heaven as a place has passed from the minds of intelligent persons, it is quite natural for us to raise the eyes in speaking of "heaven," or to point aloft when we wish to indicate the abode of the blessed. It is difficult to shake off the habitual concepts of the race, and while we know better than to suppose that there is any special "up or down" in the Cosmos, still we have the old inherited race-habit of thought which causes us to think of the higher realms of the soul as "up" toward the stars. And, in a similar manner, the old term "Astral" has persisted in occult terminology.

Once more we must caution the student against confounding the idea of the Astral Plane with the idea of place or places. There is no such place as the Astral Plane. The Astral Plane is neither up nor down, neither north, south, east or west. It lies in no special direction --- and yet it lies in all directions. It is, first, last, and always, a state or condition and not a place. It is rather a phase or degree of vibration, rather than a portion of space. Its dimensions are those of Time --- not those of Space. When we use the words: "region;" "realm;" "higher or lower; ""above or below;" we employ them merely figuratively, just as we speak of "a high rate of vibration," or "a rate or vibration above that, etc." We find it necessary to repeat this caution, for the reason that the average student falls into the pitfall of error in connecting the idea of plane with that of place, when there should be no mental association between the two.

# CHAPTER V

## AFTER DEATH

One of the questions most frequently asked by the average person who considers the question of life on "the other side," is this: "What is the experience of the soul immediately after it leaves the body?" It is somewhat pitiful to hear the answers given to this question by many of the so-called authorities on the subject. Verily, "a little knowledge is a dangerous thing."

The average person imagines that the soul simply steps out from the body and immediately enters into a new world of activity --- a wonderland of strange and mysterious scenes. To many there exists the hope of being met on the other shore by all the loved ones who have gone before --- a great reunion. While there is something which corresponds to this, there is also an entirely different condition to be experienced by the soul immediately after it passes out of the body. Let us consider the experience of the soul immediately before, and immediately after, its passage from the body, so that we may get a clearer light on the subject.

The person approaching the stage generally called "death," but which is merely a transition stage between two great planes of life, experiences a gradual dulling of the physical senses. Sight, hearing, and feeling, grow dimmer and dimmer, and the "life "of the person seems as a flickering candle flame gradually approaching utter extinction. In many cases, this is the only phenomenon attending the approach of death. But, in many other cases, while the physical senses are growing dimmer, the psychical senses are growing wonderfully acute. It is a common occurrence for dying persons to manifest a consciousness of what is occurring in another room, or another place. Clairvoyance frequently accompanies the approach of death, in some cases being attended by clairaudience, the dying person being conscious of sights and sounds in distant places.

There are also many instances recorded in the annals of the societies for psychical research, and far many more related in the privacy of family gatherings, in which the dying person has been able to so strongly project his personality that friends and relatives at a distance have actually seen his form, and in some few cases have been able to converse with him.

A careful comparison of time shows that these apparitions, in nearly every case, have appeared before the actual death of the person, rather than after it. There are, of course, cases in which a strong desire of the dying person has caused him to project his Astral body into the presence of some one near to him, immediately after death, but these cases are far more rare than those of which we have spoken above. In the majority of these cases the phenomenon is caused by a process of thought-transference of such a higher power and degree that the visited person became impressed with the consciousness of the presence of the dying friend or relative even while the soul of the latter still remained in the body.

In many cases, also, the dying person becomes psychically conscious of a nearness to loved ones who have passed on before. This, however, does not necessarily mean that these persons are actually present on the scene. One must remember that the limitations of space are largely wiped out on the Astral Plane, and that one may come into close rapport with the soul of another without there existing any near space relationship. In other words, while the two souls may not be in what may be called a nearness in space, they may nevertheless, enjoy the closest relationship in mind and spirit. It is very difficult for one still in the flesh to realize this. On the material plane, the laws of space of course govern. Telepathy gives us the key to the phenomena of "the other side." Two persons in the flesh may experience the closest relationship by means of the communion of their mental principles, and yet may be on opposite sides of the world. In the same way, two souls may enjoy the closest soul communion and communication, without the question of space nearness coming into question.

As we have said, the dying person frequently enters into soul communion and communication with those already on the other side, and is greatly cheered thereby. And this is a beautiful fact attending that which we call "death" --- this fact that there really do occur those beautiful reunion of loved ones, of which good folk discourse so hopefully.

But not in just the way these good folk usually imagine.

The dying person's Astral body gradually disengages itself from its physical counterpart. The "Astral body," as the student probably is aware, is an exact counterpart of the physical body, and during life the two dwell together in the majority of cases. The Astral body, however, leaves the physical body at the death of the latter, and forms the covering of the soul for some time. It is really a form of material substance, of a degree, however, so fine that it

22

escapes the tests which reveal ordinary matter. Toward the last the "Astral body" actually slips from the physical body and is connected with it only by a slender thread or cord of Astral substance. Finally this thread snaps, and the "Astral body" floats away, inhabited by the soul which has left the physical body behind it. But this "Astral body" is no more the soul that was the physical body which it has just left. Both physical and "Astral bodies" are merely temporary coverings for the soul itself.

The soul leaving the physical body (in the "Astral body") is plunged into a deep sleep or state of coma resembling the condition of the unborn child for several months before birth. It is being prepared for re-birth on the Astral Plane, and requires time in order to adjust itself to the new conditions and to gain strength and vigor required for its new phase of existence. Nature is full of these analogies --- birth on the physical and on the Astral Plane have many points of resemblance, and both are preceded by this period of coma. During this sleep-like stage, the soul dwells in the "Astral body" which serves as its covering and protection, just as the womb serves as the protection for the child approaching physical birth.

Before passing on, however, we should stop to consider certain features of the life of the soul in this stage. Ordinarily the soul sleeps in peace, undisturbed by, and protected from, outward influences. There are two things, however, which tend to create an exception in some cases, namely that which may be called the dreams of the sleeping soul. These dreams arise from two general classes of causes, viz: (1) intense desire filling the mind of the dying person, such as love, hate, or unfulfilled tasks or duties; (2) the strong desires and thoughts of those left behind, providing such persons are in sufficiently close rapport with the departed soul, by reason of love or other strong attachments. Either or both of these causes tend to produce a restlessness in the sleeping soul, and have a tendency to attract the soul back to the scenes of earth, either in a dreamy kind of telepathic communication, or else, in a few rare cases, by something approaching the state of somnambulism or sleep-walking of the physical life. These conditions are regrettable, for they disturb the soul and defer its evolution and development in its new phase of existence. Let us consider this in a little more detail, before passing on.

A person passing from the material into the Astral Plane in a peaceful state of mind is seldom disturbed in the Astral sleep by dream-like states. Instead, he lives naturally through the coma state and then evolves easily into the new phase of existence as naturally as the unfolding of the bud into the flower. It is different with the individual whose mind is filled with strong desires concerning earth-life, or with strong remorse, hate, or great love and anxiety for those left behind. In the latter case the poor soul is often tormented by these earthly ties, and its Astral sleep is rendered feverish and fretful. In such cases there is often also an involuntary attempt made to communicate with, or to appear to, persons still on the material plane. In extreme cases, as we have said, there may even ensue the state resembling earthly somnambulism or sleep-walking, and the poor sleeping soul may even visit its former scenes. In such cases, when the apparition is visible to men it will be noted that there is a half-awake manner and air about the apparition --- a something lacking that was present in earth-life. The history of "ghosts" bears out this statement, and the explanation just given is the only one which really throws light on the subject. In time, however, these poor earth-bound souls become tired, and finally sink into the blessed sleep which is their just lot. In the same way, the strong desires of those left behind often serves to establish a rapport condition between such persons and the departed soul, causing it to become restless and uneasy. Many a well meaning person has acted so as to retard the natural processes of the Astral Plane in relation to some loved one who has passed away, and has denied to the tired soul that rest which it has merited.

# CHAPTER VI

## THE SOUL-SLUMBER

In connection with the subject of the soul-slumber, of which we have spoken in the preceding chapter, we take the liberty of quoting from one of our earlier works, in which this subject was briefly touched upon, as follows: "The process of sinking into the restful state, and the soundness and continuance thereof, may be interfered with by those left in the earth-life. A soul which has 'something on its mind' to communicate, or which is grieved by the pain of those left behind (especially if it hears the lamentations and constant calls for its return), will fight off the dreamy state creeping over it, and will make desperate efforts to return. And, likewise, the mental calls of those who have been left behind will disturb the slumber, once it has been entered into, and will cause the sleeping soul to rouse itself and endeavor to answer the calls, or at least will partially awaken it and retard its unfoldment. These half-awake souls often manifest in spiritualistic circles. Our selfish grief and demands often cause much pain and sorrow to our loved ones who have passed over to the other side, unless they have learned the true state of affairs before they have passed out, and refuse to be called back even by those whom they love. Cases are known where souls have fought off the slumber for years in order to be around their loved ones on earth, but this course was unwise as it caused unnecessary sorrow and pain both to the one who had passed on and to those who remained on earth. We should avoid delaying by our selfish demands the progress of those who have passed on, --- let them sleep on and rest, awaiting the hour of their transformation. To do otherwise, is to make them die their death several times in succession --- those who truly love and understand always avoid this, for their love and understanding bids them let the soul depart in peace and take its well earned rest and gain its full development. This period of soul-slumber is like the existence of the babe in the mother's womb --- it sleeps that it may awaken into life and strength."

There is another phase of this particular stage of the soul progress which should be referred to here. Again we quote from what we have previously written on the subject, as follows: "It is only the soul of the person who has died a natural death which sinks at once (if not disturbed) into the soul-slumber. Those who die by accident, or who are killed --- in other words, those who pass out of the body suddenly, find themselves wide-awake and in full possession or their mental faculties for some time. They often are not aware that they have 'died' and cannot understand what is the matter with them. They are often fully conscious (for a short time) of life on earth, and can see and hear all that is going on around them, by means of their Astral senses. They cannot realize that they have passed out of the body, and are often sorely perplexed. Their lot would be most unhappy for a few days, until the sleep finally overcame them in due course, were it not for the Astral Helpers, those blessed souls from the higher states of existence, who gather around them and gently break to them the news of their real condition, and offer them words of comfort and advise, and generally 'take care' of them until they sink into the soul-slumber just as a tired child sinks to sleep at night. These Helpers never fail in their duty, and no one who passes out suddenly, be he or she 'good' or 'bad' is neglected, for these helpers know that all are Gods children and their own spiritual brothers and sisters. Men of high spiritual development and powers have been known to pass out of their physical bodies, temporarily (dwelling in their Astral bodies), for the purpose of giving aid and advice in time of great catastrophes (such as the Johnstown Flood and the Titanic ' Disaster) or after a great battle, when immediate advice and assistance were needed. . . . Persons dying in the way of which we have spoken, of course gradually fall into the slumber of the soul, just as in the cases of those dying a natural death."

Life reviews

Another matter which should be mentioned in this place is that wonderful phenomenon of the review of the past life of the soul, that great panorama which passes before the mental vision of the soul as it sinks into the soul slumber. This the authorities inform us really occupies but an infinitesimal moment of time --- a moment so brief that it can scarcely be spoken of as a point in time. Yet in this brief moment, the soul witnesses the panorama of the life it has passed on earth. Scene after scene, of infancy to old age, passes before it in review. The most insignificant incident is reproduced with as much fidelity to detail as is the greatest event. The subconscious planes of memory unfold their secrets to the last --- nothing is reserved or withheld. Moreover, the soul, by its awakened spiritual discernment, is able to know the meaning, cause, and consequence of every event in its life. It is able to analyze and to pass judgment upon itself and its acts. Like an omniscient and impartial judge it judges itself. The result of this process is that the acts of one's past life are concentrated and impressed upon the records of the soul, there to become as seeds which will produce better fruit in the future. These seeds serve to bear the fruits of future character, in future lives, at least, so far as the acquired characteristics and desires will admit of.

To those who may object that it is impossible for the mind to grasp the

26

events of a lifetime in the space of a moment of time, we would say that psychology will inform them that even in ordinary earth-life this is possible.

For there are many recorded cases in which a person nodding into slumber has dreamed of events which have occupied an apparent period of many years. In ordinary dreams time is practically reduced to a small unit, and in the state of which we speak the process of concentration is intensified, and the single point of time covers the period of the longest life.

The soul carries with it into its slumber state a concentrated record of its entire life, including the seeds of its desires, ambitions, likes and dislikes, attractions and repulsions. These seed-ideas soon begin to sprout and bear blossom and fruit. Not only in future incarnations are these manifest, but also in the life of the soul on the Astral Plane. For kind Nature does not impose on the soul the task of living out and outliving all of its tendencies in future incarnations, but so arranges that many of these strong impulses shall be manifested and worn out on the Astral Plane, so that the soul may leave them behind when it is re-born into a new earth-life. And it is toward this fruition that the soul-slumber serves. During the soul-sleep the soul is prepared for its entrance into Astral life and manifestation, the details of which we shall see as we proceed. The soul-slumber is just as necessary for the soul in this stage of its progress, as is the slumber of the unborn babe in the womb of its mother.

We have heard of some unreasoning persons who, upon being made acquainted with these teachings, manifested a fear of the soul slumber state, and who said they "feared the sleep in an unknown place, among so many unknown things and creatures." This objection seems very childish to the advanced occultist, for he knows that there is nowhere in Nature in which an entity is so carefully and fully guarded as in this case of the sleeping soul on the great Astral Plane. So absolutely secure from invasion or intrusion, from harm or hurtful influence, are these sleeping souls that nothing short of a complete revolution of Nature's most sacred laws could affect them. The abode is not a place, remember, but a condition or state. And this state or condition is such that no malign or harmful influence could in any way whatsoever reach or even draw near them. Would that all of us in earth-life were so securely guarded. So secure are these sleeping souls that it would seem as if all of Nature's forces had conspired to guard and protect them. It is a Hindu maxim which runs as follows: 'Not even the gods on their high thrones have any power or dominion over the sleeping souls. "

To those whose ideals on the subject of "the other side" have been so influenced by the teachings of current theology that this conception of the soul-slumber may seem strange and unusual, we would say that a little consideration will show that under the popular conceptions of even the most favored theologies will be found many veiled allusions to this blessed state of rest which the soul so sadly requires after one strenuous life and before another. "He giveth His beloved sleep;" "There is rest for the weary , ""He has gone to his long rest , "these and many other familiar expressions and quotations seek to express the innate idea implanted in the human mind regarding a period of rest which shall come to the tired soul. The idea Of "rest," after the stress and storms of life, is so natural and instinctive that it may be said to represent the strongest inclination and conviction of the human soul in connection with the idea of death. It is as fixed as is the conviction of future life beyond the grave. In the advanced occult teachings alone, however, are to be found the explanation of the idea.

The soul which is instructed regarding the existence and nature of this period of soul slumber will find nothing but satisfaction in the contemplation thereof. It will learn to regard this stage of its future existence as a blessed balm and comfort. It will feel toward this state that which we find expressed in the words of the old song: "And calm and peaceful do I sleep, rocked in the Cradle of the Deep." As rest, securely resting, on the bosom of that Great Ocean of Life. Rest, calm, peace, security, protection --- this is the condition of the soul-slumber on the Astral Plane.

# CHAPTER VII

## THE SOUL'S AWAKENING

There is a great difference in the time required for the development in soul-slumber by different souls. Some dwell in this state for a very short time, while souls of a higher degree of attainment require a much longer time in the soul-slumber state. Here, too, we find a remarkable correspondence with the phenomenon of gestation and birth on the material plane, which should be considered by the student. For instance, in the case of these animals whose natural life period is short, we find, as a rule, that their period of gestation in the womb is correspondingly short; on the other hand, animals of a natural long life spend a much longer period in the womb before birth. Thus, the elephant has twenty or twenty-one months in the womb; man, nine months; rabbits, one month; guinea-pigs, three weeks; the natural life of each bearing a relation to the period of gestation. In the same way, the gestation period on the Astral Plane --- the period of the soul slumber is found to vary in proportion to the time the awakened soul is to pass on the Astral Plane. An apparent exception to this rule is found in the case of persons of highly advanced spiritual power and knowledge, in which the soul is able, by its knowledge and power, to largely control the natural processes instead of being under their general control.

The difference in the period of soul-slumber in varying cases, above noted, arises from the fact that the soul during its slumber period discards the lower portions of its mental nature (as well as its Astral body) and awakens only when it has reached the highest state of development possible for it, when it is able to pass on to the particular plane or sub-plane for which its degree of development calls. A soul of low development has very little to "shed" in this way, and soon awakens on a low plane. A soul of higher development, on the contrary, must shed and discard sheath after sheath of the lower mental and animal nature, before it can awaken on the plane of its highest attainment. When we say "shed" or discard, we mean rather prepare to shed or discard, for the actual process of discarding or shedding these lower fragments of personality occurs immediately after the first stage of the awakening, as we shall see in the next paragraph.

The soul feeling the impulses of re-awakened life, stirs itself slowly and languidly, as one does in awakening from a sound slumber in earth-life. Then, like the butterfly throwing aside the chrysalis shell, it slips away from

29

the Astral body, and in rapid succession unconsciously discards the lower principles of its nature. This occupies but a short time, and occurs while the soul is slowly regaining consciousness. At the moment of the actual awakening, the soul is free from all these worn out shells and encumbrances, and opens its eyes upon the scenes of its new activities and existence in the Astral World.

Each soul is destined to dwell on the plane of the highest and best in itself, after the dross of the lower elements has been discarded. It awakens on the plane in which the highest and best in itself is given a chance to develop and expand. The soul may, and often does, make great progress on the Astral Plane, and during its stay there, may discard more of its lower nature as it passes to higher and still higher planes or sub-planes.

It is a beautiful fact this of the soul dwelling on the plane of its highest and best. The student immediately recognizes that this answers the longing of the soul, and the aspiration of the heart. There is often something within individuals which is much higher and better than their everyday life and actions would seem to indicate. Material environment and circumstances tend to retard and prevent the expression of the best in us, in many cases. Therefore, it is pleasant to know that on "the other side" the soul is relieved of all that tends to hold it back and drag it down, and is rendered free to express and develop those qualities and characteristics which represent the best and truest that is in it. This fact accords not only with the sense of justice and equity; not only with the longings and cravings of the imprisoned soul, but also with the facts and principles of evolution, which ever attracts upward and onward, toward some far off goal of attainment and perfection.

If passing on the plane of its future activities, the soul has discarded its Astral body, that strange counterpart of the physical body is discarded still further back. Henceforth the soul does not wear the form and shape of the human being, but is something of a far higher order of being to which the terms "shape" and "form" do not apply. Our physical bodies (and their Astral counterparts) are the result of physical evolution, and are but the bodies of developed animals. The soul on the higher planes has no need of arms and legs, hands and feet, --- it dwells where these instruments of a lower form of expression are not needed. It is a being transcending the limitations of physical life.

The discarded mental principles soon are resolved into their original ele-

30

ments (but the discarded Astral body becomes what is known as an "Astral shell," and, forsaken by its former occupant it sinks, by what may be called astral gravitation, to the lowest planes of the Astral, there to slowly disintegrate. The lower planes of the Astral are filled with these discarded Astral shells, floating about in the Astral atmosphere. They are not pleasant things to see, and happily the soul on the other side does not witness them, for it dwells on a plane far above their region.

But persons in earth-life who dapple in things physical, before they understand the first principles of psychic science, often find themselves on the lower planes of the Astral Plane and consequently witness some very unpleasant sights in this region, as might be expected.

The plane upon which the soul awakens is not a place, you remember, but a state or condition of existence --- a degree in the scale of the vibratory energy of the spiritual world. As we have said, each soul awakens on the plane representing its highest and best, upon which plane it dwells during its stay on the Astral Plane, excepting where it develops itself and moves on to a still higher plane, or, when, as alas! sometimes happens, it longs for the fleshpots of Egypt and is attracted by memories of lower principles and descends to a lower plane where it finds more congenial company and surroundings. There is naturally a great difference between the various planes and sub-planes of the Astral Plane. Some are very little removed from the low scenes of earth-life, while others express the highest conceptions of the human soul. And each attracts to itself those who are fitted to dwell in its region --- those whose best and highest correspond with the new environment. But the highest and best of the soul of low development is but very little above the everyday thoughts and actions of the same soul in the body. Persons of low spiritual development must needs go through many periods of purification and development before they can escape the lure and attraction of the material world. There are souls so earth-bound --- so hypnotized by the low pleasures of earth life --- that on "the other side" they even refuse to forsake their Astral shells, and actually strive to abide in the worn-out and disintegrating shells while they last, and maintain a rapport condition with the scenes and associates of the former life. Others find themselves on planes in which there is a conflict between the upward attraction of the higher things 'of spiritual life and the lower things of the material world, and they live a more or less unbalanced life in the Astral, at least for a time, until one attraction proves the stronger and they rise and fall in the spiritual scale, in accordance therewith. Others still find themselves on a plane in which there is but little or no attraction from the material world, and to them the Astral Life is lived out in advancement, development, and a fuller expression of the highest and best within them.

The awakening of the soul is akin to a new birth --- an entrance into a new world of experience. The soul manifests no fear of its new surroundings, but is full of activity in the direction of expression and manifestation of its new powers. There is much to occupy the soul, as we shall see as we proceed. It is not lonely or lonesome, for it has the companionship of those in harmony and sympathy with itself, and is free from the enharmony and friction of association with those of different natures. It finds opportunity for the fullest expression of its activities and desires, and, particularly on the higher planes, finds life much happier than on the material plane. Only the souls of the lowest development --- those poor earth-bound creatures --- are unhappy, for they are removed from the only thing which gives them pleasure, the things of earth. And even in their cases there is at least something like happiness at times.

After the soul-slumber, the soul awakens into LIFE, not into a region of Death. Like the butterfly, it spreads its wings and enjoys its new state of existence, and does not mourn the loss of the chrysalis form and life. In the succeeding chapters you will see the nature and incidents of this new life, in further detail.

# CHAPTER VIII

## ASTRAL PLANE GEOGRAPHY

Before proceeding to a consideration of the experiences of the newly awakened disembodied soul, we ask you to take a brief glimpse at what may be
called "geography" of the Astral Plane, that great scene or plane of the activities of the disembodied souls of the race this is the logical path of approach
to the subject. For, before we are asked to consider the inhabitants of a new
country, we are generally made acquainted with the country itself, its hills
and valleys, its rivers and plains, its highlands and lowlands. And, using the
same figure of speech, let us now take a little lesson in the geography of the
Astral Plane, the place of abode of the disembodied souls.

But, first let us again remind you that the Astral Plane is not a country --- is
not a place at all --- in the usual sense. Its dimensions are not those of space,
but of vibration. In a way it may be said that the dimensions of the Astral
Plane are the dimensions of Time, for vibrations can be measured only by
their rate of motion, and that rate is determined only in terms of Time. The
same is true of all vibrations whether of Astral energy or the lower forms of
energy. The vibrations of light are measured in terms of Time, that is to say
so many vibrations to the second, and so on. The higher the rate of vibration,
the greater the rate of speed manifested in the vibration. The ancient occultists were fond of stating the truth regarding the highest forms of vibration,
by saying that there a rate of vibration so infinitely rapid that it seems to be
absolutely still and motionless. From this extreme, we descend by degrees
until the very grossest forms of matter are reached, and there we find a rate
of vibration so slow that it likewise seems motionless.

The substance of the Astral Plane is, of course, very much finer than that of
the material plane --- its vibrations very much higher than the finest form of
material substance. But there is the widest range between the vibrations of
the lowest planes and those of the higher ones. In fact, the difference between the lowest plane of the Astral, and the highest of the material plane,
is less than the difference between the lowest and highest of the Astral itself.
So that between these two extremes of Astral vibrations, we have the same
great territory that we would have on the material plane, with this difference,
however, that the material territory is measured by space dimensions, while
that of the Astral is to be measured only in terms of vibration, or time, and
not of space.

For instance, when one travels on the material plane, he must traverse space --- feet, yards, or miles. But, on the Astral Plane, when one travels he traverses rates of vibrations --- that is to say, he passes from a high rate of vibration to a lower, or vice versa. And these various planes or sub-planes of vibratory energy constitute the geographical features of the Astral Plane. There are countless planes and sub-planes, or "regions" of the Astral Plane, which may be traveled, but all Astral travel is performed simply by passing from one degree of vibration to another. Using a crude example, we may say that it is somewhat akin to passing from the state of ice to that of water, and then of steam. Or, again, it may be thought of as passing from ordinary atmospheric air, to liquid air, and then to solid air (the latter is theoretically possible, although science has not yet been able to solidify air. These illustrations are of course very crude, but they may help you to understand the geography of the Astral Plane a little better.

Henceforth, we shall speak of travel on the Astral Plane --- that is travel between the different planes and sub-planes of the Astral as if it were on the material plane. That is to say, instead of saying that the soul passes from one state of vibration to another, we shall speak of it as proceeding from one subplane or plane to another, in the same terms that we would employ in describing a journey on the material plane. This will simplify matters for us, and will obviate a needless repetition of the statement regarding vibrational conditions or states. With this understanding, we shall now proceed.

There are many states or conditions of existence on the Astral Plane, which are spoken of as planes and sub-planes. These planes and sub-planes are inhabited by souls fitted to dwell upon the particular series of planes or sub-planes upon which they awaken from the soul-slumber. Subtle principles of soul attraction draw each soul to the particular place for which it is fitted. The great law of attraction operates unerringly here. There is no chance or haphazard about the mechanism of the law of attraction. The law operates with absolute precision and uniformity --- it makes no mistakes.

Each soul is restricted in its range by its own inherent limitations and degrees of development. There is no need of Astral policemen to keep the disembodied souls in their rightful places. It is impossible for the disembodied soul to travel into planes above its own immediate series. The law of vibration prevents this. But, on the contrary, each and every soul may, if it so chooses, freely visit the planes and sub-planes beneath its own series, and freely witness the scenery and phenomena of those lower planes and

34

mingle with the inhabitants thereof. (This entirely apart from the high form of telepathic communication which prevails between disembodied souls on the Astral Plane.) This is a very wise provision of the Law, for were it otherwise the higher planes Would be open to the influence of those dwelling on the lower, and the soul-life and development would be interrupted, just as a class-room in a school of philosophy might be interrupted by a gang of hoodlums from the slums of a large city. (For, remember, the Astral Plane has its slums and hoodlums, as well as the material plane.)

In a previous work we gave a somewhat crude, but nevertheless a very striking illustration of this matter of the intercommunication between the various planes and subplans of the Astral Plane, which we herewith reproduce, as follows: "It is absolutely impossible for a soul to go beyond the plane to which it belongs, although those on the upper planes may freely revisit the lower planes, this being the rule of the Astral Plane --- not an arbitrary law, but a law of nature. If the student will pardon the commonplace comparison, he may get an understanding of it by' imagining a large screen, or series of screens, such as are used for sorting coal into sizes. The large coal is caught by the first screen, the next size by the second, and so on until the tiny coal is reached. Now, the large coal cannot get into the receptacle of the smaller sizes, but the small sizes may easily pass through the screen and join the large sizes, if force be imparted to them. Just so on the Astral Plane, the soul with the greatest amount of materiality, and coarsest nature, is stopped by the screen of a certain grade or plane, and cannot pass on to the higher ones while one which has passed on to the higher planes, having cast off more confining sheaths, can easily pass backward and forward among the lower planes, if it so desires. In fact, souls often do so, for the purpose of visiting friends on the lower planes, and giving them enjoyment and comfort, and, in case of a highly developed soul, much spiritual help may be given in this way, by means of advice and instruction, when the soul on the lower plane is ready to receive it."

In the passage alluded to above, there is the following additional words, which also should be repeated here, for it concerns the geography of the Astral Plane. We allude to the following: "The one exception to the rule of free passage to the planes below that of the particular soul, is the one which prevents the lower-plane souls from entering the 'plane of the sleepers,' which plane may not be entered by souls which have awakened on a low plane, but which may be freely entered by those pure and exalted souls who have attained a high place. The plane of soul-slumber is sacred to those occupying

35

it, and those higher souls just mentioned, and it is in fact rather of the nature of a distinct and separate state than one of the great series of planes and sub plans."

There are as many different kind of regions on the Astral Plane as there are on the material plane, and each plane is inhabited by exactly the class of souls which it might be expected to attract. There are to be found the abodes of degraded souls, so steeped in materiality and animality, that they would be veritable hell to a soul of higher attainment. It may well be imagined that the soul of higher impulses has no desire to travel into these depths of the Astral, unless, indeed it be some very highly developed soul which is willing to "descend into hell" in order to minister to the needs of some lower soul which is striving to emerge from the slough of despond into which its earth life has thrown it. Such ministering spirits do exist, and perform this work for their lower brothers and sisters. But, as a rule, the disembodied souls prefers to work out its own evolution on its own plane, that it may ascend to the higher grades of spiritual opportunity in its next incarnation, and that it may aquire spiritual knowledge during its sojourn on its particular plane of the Astral.

# CHAPTER IX

## PRIMITIVE SOUL-STATES

The man and woman of culture and refinement are generally inclined to smile at the heaven-traditions of the primitive peoples, and, perhaps, to experience a feeling of sorrow at the lowly ideals of the barbarous and semi-barbarous races of man as manifested by their primitive conceptions regarding the heaven-world. But, the experienced occultist, in turn, may smile at the smug complacency of many of those in civilized lands who speak pityingly of these lowly ideals and conceptions, for these occultists know that these conceptions have a basis in reality in the life of the primitive peoples on the Astral Plane.

Just as the future condition of the individual is determined largely by the nature, character and strength of his desires, so is his life on the Astral Plane largely determined by his desires and ideals. The Astral Plane gives free expression to the ideals entertained by the individual in earth-life, and, in fact, may be spoken of as largely a reflection of those ideals. On the Astral Plane our ideals tend toward a real manifestation. And this is true not only of high ideals, but of the lowest as well.

This fact being understood, it will be seen that it is a logical necessity that the astral existence of the primitive peoples of the race shall be a reflection of the ideals and desires held by them during the period of earth life --- a dramatization of their desire-ideals of their past life. In short, the Indian really finds his "happy hunting grounds," and the other primitive peoples their particular paradise as pictured in their creeds and faiths. This at first, seems somewhat shocking to the person whose ideals of "heaven" are modeled upon the realm of golden streets, where milk and honey flows. But a little thought will show that the conception of the "golden streets" is but a little higher in the scale than that of the "happy hunting-ground," for it is purely material and reflects the ideals of a race whose desires are for glittering and costly things.

If one will but consider the emotional and intellectual nature of the primitive person, he will see that to surround such a soul with the environment of the cultured civilized person would be to render him very unhappy. In fact, such a heaven would to him seem like a hell. One has but to imagine a savage in earth life placed in a palace with the surroundings fitted to the ideals of a person of high culture and refinement, to realize just how miserable the savage would really be. The same thing holds true on the Astral Plane. Nature is kind to the savage, as well as to the cultured person, and furnishes him with the environment in which he will feel the most at home, and in which he will find the greatest opportunity for self-expression.

This does not mean that on the Astral Plane there are elaborately arranged series of scenery and surroundings fitted for the tastes of each and every kind of soul. On the contrary, there is no such stage-setting whatsoever. Here is the secret: There is no scenery on the Astral Plane except that furnished by the thought-forms of the souls inhabiting it. Each soul carries his own set of scenery with it, in his imaginative faculties of mind. It follows, of course, that many souls of the same general ideals and tastes inhabiting the same sub-plane, will carry the same mental scenery with them. And, as the power of thought-transference is manifested strongly on the Astral Plane, each soul affects the general scenery of the others. In fact, the scenery of each sub-plane, or division thereof, represents the composite ideals and mental images of those inhabiting it. In earth-life, environment largely makes the man --- on the Astral Plane, man makes his own environment, in accordance with the absolute and unvarying laws of Nature.

The Indian, during the short period of his sojourn on the Astral Plane, finds himself surrounded by all that makes life pleasant and harmonious for him. The clairvoyants among the old American Indians, who were able to penetrate the lower planes of the Astral Plane, were thoughtful when they reported the existence of "the happy hunting grounds" of their departed brothers on "the other side." True also were the reports of the shadowy forms which communicated with their former brothers on earth, to the same effect. The heaven-world of the Red Indian was precisely as his medicine-men had taught him it would be. Such a soul, awakening from the soul slumber, would find itself perfectly at home, surrounded by all that made life pleasant to it great forests and plains, streams and rivers, plenty of buffalo and deer to be shot, and plenty of fish to be caught. All these things existed for such. But they existed only mentally. Like a very intense dream these things appeared to such a soul --- but it never realized that it was merely a dream. "Dreams are true while they last," as the old writings inform us. And, as for that, the wisest of the race inform us that the phenomenal universe is really in the nature of a Dream of the Absolute --- but it is none the less real to us. Even in earth life, we sometimes experience dreams so real that we suffer as keenly, or enjoy as rapturously, in them, as if they were the only somewhat more substantial realities of the waking state.

Those who have made a study of the subject, inform us that among all races of men there are many reports of clairvoyants, seers, dreamers, and communicators with departed souls, who assert positively the existence of "heavens" in exact accordance with the religious teachings of their tribe or race, no matter how crude and barbarous these conceptions may appear to one of a more cultured faith. It is very easy to dismiss these reports either as pure inventions, or dreams of the priests. But, closer examination will reveal the fact that there is a striking basic unity among them --- they all agree on the fundamental points, although they differ as to the details. The occultist knows that these reports are all truthful, so far as they go, and have been based on actual physic experiences of certain members of the tribe of people. Although they differ greatly in details, they agree in fundamentals, and are all based on truth. A little consideration of the nature of the Astral phenomena, as we have stated it, will explain the matter.

These primitive souls spend a brief existence on the lower Astral Planes to which they have been attached, and develop newer and fuller ideals and desires, which will blossom and bear fruit in their next earth-incarnation. Moreover, they wear-out and outlive certain of their lower desires and ideals, and in this way, make way for the spiritual evolution which is ever seeking to unfold on the Astral; serves to unfold these souls a little --- only a very little, it is true --- but every little is a gain. Moreover, as the Astral Life (and usually the earth-life) of the savage is comparatively brief, these souls really make considerable progress in a given space of time --- they may live a hundred earth lives, and the corresponding Astral Life, while a more highly developed soul is earning its spiritual rest on the higher Astral planes. Compensation and equity is found here, as elsewhere, in the life-processes.

One of the great gains of the savage soul on the Astral Plane is that of the development of comradeship and fellow-feeling. This is caused by the reunion of the soul with its friends of earth-life, and the joy felt thereat. Moreover, the animosities of earth life are softened by the nature of the life on the Astral, for with a bounteous supply of all that the savage soul craves, there is far less opportunity for jealousy and rivalry than on earth. And, accordingly, hate is stilled, and comradeship and elementary friendship (the buddings of universal love) are encouraged. Each trip to the Astral Plane burns out a little more of the lower nature, and awakens a little more of the higher --- otherwise, there would be no progress for the race in repeated lives. Each soul, no matter how undeveloped it may be, learns a little more of that feeling of unity and oneness, each time it is relieved of the stress of the physical body. So that, we may see, that even in these crude "heavens" of the primitive peoples, there is the opportunity and the certainty of progress. Happiness begets Love, and the soul responds to the stimulus.

The primitive soul abides but a short time on the Astral Plane to which it is attached. It soon wears out its limited opportunity for expression (although to the soul itself, eternities seem to have been passed). It soon feels the drowsiness of the sleep, which precedes rebirth overtaking it, and falling into a state of coma, it awaits the attraction of Karma which shortly leads it into a new body, to again study the lessons of life, and to live and out-live that which it finds within itself. The attraction of earth-life is strong in such a soul, and the law of attraction soon draws it back to the scenes of earth. There is no injustice or harshness in this --- each soul gets that which it most desires, and that for which it most craves. The Law of Compensation is in full force here, as elsewhere, and eternal Justice reigns. "All is well," even with such lowly souls --- and they are all on THE PATH!

# CHAPTER X

## ASTRAL RELIGIOUS EXPERIENCES

The student of comparative religions is struck with the fact that from the primal stock of religious belief there emerges an almost countless number of creeds, sects, and divisions of religious thought. From the very primitive superstitions of the simple races to the most advanced conceptions of the cultured peoples, there runs a uniting thread of fundamental belief in a SOMETHING which is above the phenomenal universe, and which is the Causeless Cause of the Universe. Coupled with this conception we find the fundamental belief that the soul survives after the death of the body. But this conception, also, is variously interpreted by the different religious authorities and sects. The third general conception, the fundamental religious instinct of the race, is that which holds that the future life of the soul depends upon the character and actions of the individual during his earth-life.

It is a long journey from some of the most primitive interpretations of these three fundamental principles of religious belief, to that high conception of the advanced occultists which has been stated by a gifted author as follows:

"There are three truths which are absolute, and which cannot be lost, but yet may remain silent for lack of speech. (1) The soul of man is immortal, and its future is the future of a thing whose growth and splendor have no limit. (2) The principle which gives life dwells in us, and without us; is undying and eternally beneficent; is not heard or seen, or felt, but is perceived by the man who desires perception. (3) Each man is his own absolute law-giver; the dispenser of glory or gloom to himself, the decreer of his life, his reward, his punishment. These truths, which are as great as his life itself, are as simple as the simplest mind of man. Feed the hungry with them."

Yet each of the conceptions, and all the varying degrees which appear between them, are alike the result of man's intuitive perception of that SOMETHING; the Immortality of the Soul; and the Law of Karma. The difference between the varying forms of religious thought is simply the differences between the conceptions of Truth formed by the minds of various religious leaders or teachers and their followers.

All creeds and religious dogmas are man-made, as the enemies of revealed religion maintain. But, these good folks miss the other half of the truth, i.

41

e. that underlying the man-made creeds and dogmas eternally exists the intuitive perception of the race regarding the existence of Truth. The mind may not be able to correctly interpret the intuitive perception, but it finds itself positively impressed by the fact that Truth does exist. Man has made a god of nearly everything in the material world, and has fallen down and worshipped his own creation --- this because of his limited power of inter-pretation. But in worshipping the stick or stone, the graven image, or the anthropomorphic deities, he was unconsciously, and in reality, worshipping that SOMETHING which was the cause of the religious intuition within his soul. And, as one of the Hindu Vedas beautifully states it, the Supreme One accepts all such worship, when honestly given as intended for itself. "Truth is but One, although men call it by many names," says the old Yogi sage of centuries past.

Each man creates for himself, and holds to, the particular form of religious faith which is best suited for the requirements of his soul at any particular period of its evolution. When he is ready for a higher conception, he sheds and discards the old belief and eagerly embraces the newer one. The world has witnessed many instances of this evolution of religious thought, and, indeed, it is really going through an important one at this particular time. The path of the race is strewn with broken and discarded idols, material and mental, which were once precious to millions of worshippers. And, as the race advances, many more idols will be overthrown and left crumbling on the paths of time. But each idol had its own appropriate place in the general history of the evolution of the religious thought of the race. Each served its purpose, and its ideals served to aid man in his perpetual and eternal journey toward Absolute Truth.

In view of the above-stated facts, would we not naturally expect to find in a rational and equitable adjustment of conditions on "the other side" some provision made for the sincere religious faiths and beliefs of the race, differ-ing from each other as these faiths and beliefs may be? Imagine the spiritual anguish of a disembodied soul were it to see the cherished beliefs of an earnest life, and the traditions of many generations of ancestors, swept away as by a flood. And, this, particularly in view of the fact that the soul would not be sufficiently advanced to understand or accept the higher forms of re-ligious truth, but would be merely asked to accept either something which it could not understand, or else which was repugnant to it by reason of its past training and experience. Such would be cruelty to the disembodied soul as much as if the same thing were attempted during its earth-life.

There is a native belief among many persons which would imply that the disembodied soul is magically, and instantaneously transformed from ignorance into absolute knowledge upon passing over to "the other side." This is a childlike belief, and has no basis in fact. There is really but very little difference in the general intelligence or spiritual attainment of the soul, before or after death. Soul progress is gradual, in or out of the body. The disembodied soul is practically the same in general intelligence and understanding, in and out of the body. "In" and "out" of the body are but successive phases of its continuous life, succeeding each other like day and night, summer and winter. Therefore, what is true of a particular soul's feelings and emotions in earth-life is almost equally true of the same things in its life in the Astral. We mention this that you may better understand that to which we have been leading up in the previous pages of this chapter.

Accordingly, what we might naturally expect to find (according to reason and in equity) regarding the religious experiences of the disembodied soul, is so in fact. That is to Say, on the Astral Plane each soul finds itself surrounded by a religious environment in accordance with the best of the beliefs entertained by it in its earth-life. It will not only find the particular heavens, or hells, which it expected to find, but it will also find itself in contact with other souls of a similar belief, and with the prophets and sages and founders of its own religion. But this environment will be of the nature of a mirage, for it is a product of human thought and has no counterpart in the absolute facts of nature. The thought-forms of a particular form of religious thought gather great strength on the Astral Plane, and endure with all the appearance of permanent reality to the perception and understanding of the believer and devotee --- although entirely invisible to those of a different faith. The presence of prophets and founders remains with the environment, though the souls of these individuals have long since passed on to other planes of life. The Astral Plane is a realm of ideals, and each soul finds its ideals realized thereon.

The good Christian finds a manifestation of the best in his own creed and beliefs, and rests fully assured that he has had the true faith, and has reaped the reward he expected. But, the same is true of the good Brahmin, or the good Mohammedan, or the good Confucian. Moreover, each particular sect or division of religious belief finds a corroboration of its own beliefs on the Astral Plane. But there is no warring of sects or religions. Each soul finds its own, and is oblivious of the rest. But, note this apparent exception: the soul which has advanced far enough to realize that there is Truth in all religious beliefs, and which has manifested a tolerant spirit in earth-life, is also given a corroboration of his belief, and is allowed to see the joys of the blessed of all religious faiths.

It must be remembered, however, that these Astral representations of the various religious faiths and beliefs comprise only the best of each particular form of belief --- in short, the soul witnesses the highest conception and ideal of which it is capable regarding its favorite religion. This naturally has the effect and result of developing the highest religious conceptions in the soul, and inhibiting the lower ones, to the end that when the soul undertakes its next earthly pilgrimage it will carry with it a taste and inclination for only the highest in its own religion, and will thus aid in the evolution of religion on earth. Sometimes a soul will evolve from one form of religious conception in its Astral Life, and upon its reincarnation will be ready for one higher. Remember, always, that the spiritual evolution constantly leads onward and upward, from lower to higher --- on, and on, and on, forever.

The question of religious rewards and punishments, on the Astral Plane, which naturally forms a part of the subject just considered, will be discussed in the following chapter.

# CHAPTER XI

## ASTRAL HEAVENS AND HELLS

In the quotation from the occult writer, given in the preceding chapter, the following statement is made: "Each man is his own absolute law-giver, the dispenser of glory or gloom to himself, the decreer of his life, his reward, his punishment." And this is true not only in earth-life, but also doubly true of the life of the soul on the Astral Plane. For each disembodied soul carries with it its own heaven or hell, of its own creation, and of its favorite belief, and partakes of the blessings or sorrows of each, according to its merits. But the Judge who sentences it to reward or punishment is not a Power outside of itself, but a Power Within --- in short, its own conscience. On the Astral Plane the conscience of the soul asserts itself very forcibly, and the still, quiet voice, that was perhaps smothered during earth-life, now speaks in trumpet-like tones, and the soul hears and obeys.

A man's own conscience, when allowed to speak clearly and forcibly, is the most severe Judge that exists. Stripping aside all self-deception, and hypoc-risy, conscious or unconscious, it causes the soul to stand forth naked and bare to its own spiritual gaze. And the soul, speaking as its own conscience, sentences itself in accordance with its own conceptions of right and wrong, and accepts its fate as merited and just. Man can fly from the judgment of others --- but he can never escape from his own conscience on the Astral Plane. He finds himself unable to escape from the judgment seat of con-science, and he leads himself away to his reward or punishment. Such is the poetic justice of Nature, which far exceeds any conception of mortal man in his religious speculations.

And, note the absolute equity and justice of it all. Man is judged according to the highest standards of his own soul, which, of course, represent the standards of his time and environment. The best in himself --- the highest of which he is capable --- judges and passes upon all in him below that stan-dard. The result of this is that what the highest reason conceives as absolute justice is meted out by the soul to itself. The leading thinkers of the race almost unanimously agree that any arbitrary standard of punishment, such as is expressed by the criminal codes of the race, must necessarily fall far short of meting out invariable actual justice. For the environment and education of the criminal may have been such that the commission of the crime is almost natural to him while the same crime, committed by another, would be the result of a direct betrayal of his conscience and a breaking of a moral law of which he is fully aware and conscious. We would hardly call it criminal for the fox to steal a chicken, or for the cat slyly to lap milk from the bowl on the table. There are many human beings whose sense of moral right and wrong is but little above that of the above named animals. Therefore, even human law, at least theoretically aims not to punish, but to restrain by example and precept.

In connection with the thought expressed in the preceding paragraph, we must remember that absolute justice has no place for punishment as such. As we have said, theoretically at least, even human law does not seek to punish the criminal, but merely seeks the following ends, viz: (1) To warn others not to commit a like crime (2) to restrain the criminal from committing further crime, by confining him, or by imposing other deterring penalties (3) to reform the criminal by pointing out the advantages of right action and the disadvantage of wrong action. This being true even of finite human law, what should we expect of infinite cosmic law, in this particular? Surely, nothing more or less than a discipline which should encourage the unfoldment of the "good" qualities of the soul, and the smothering of the "evil" ones. And this is just what the advanced occultist does find to exist on the Astral Plane.

In this connection, it must be remembered that the discipline which would appeal most to the soul of lowly ideals, would be without avail in the case of the cultured soul --- and vice versa. In short, it may truthfully be said that the nature of the appropriate discipline in each individual case is well expressed by the ideal of heaven and hell entertained by the individual in earth-life, and which ideal, of course, remains with the soul after it has passed from the body to the Astral Plane. The mind of certain individuals is fully satisfied with the ideals of a lake of brimstone for sinners, and the pleasant abode in a golden-streeted heaven, with accompaniments of harp and crown, for the blessed. Others, far advanced beyond this stage, having left behind them the old ideas of a heaven in space and a hell of torment, think that the greatest happiness possible to themselves would be a state or condition in which they could see their ideals made real, their highest aims realized, their dreams come true; and their greatest punishment a condition in which they could follow up to its logical result the evil they have done. And, both of these classes of souls find on the Astral Plane the heavens and hells of which they have thought --- for both have created their heaven or hell from the material of their own inner consciousness. And such mental conceptions lack nothing of reality to those who are conscious of them --- the joy and suffering lose nothing of effect by reason of the absence of the physical body.

On the Astral Plane, the "sinner" who believes in a hell of brimstone and flames, which awaits him by reason of "the foul crimes done in his days of nature," is not disappointed.

His beliefs supply the necessary environment, and his conscience condemns him to the punishment in which he believes. Even if he has sought to disbe-lieve these things by the use of his reason, and still retains the subconscious memories of his childhood teachings or the traditions of his race, he will find himself in the same condition. He will undergo the traditional tortures and suffering (all in his imagination of course) until he receives a valuable disci-plinary lesson, the dim memories of which will haunt him in the next incar-nation. This, of course, is an extreme case. There are many other degrees and grades of "hells" carried over to the Astral Plane by souls of various shades of religious belief. Each has the punishment which is best adapted to exert a deterring influence and effect over him in his next life.

The same is true of the ideal of "heaven," The soul finds itself enjoying the bliss of the blessed, according to its own ideals, for the good deeds and acts it has to its credit in the infallible books of its memory. Inasmuch as no soul has been altogether "bad," nor none absolutely "good," it follows that each soul has a taste both of reward and punishment, according to its merits as determined by its awakened conscience. Or, stating it in another way, the conscience "strikes an average" for it, which average, likewise, agrees in detail with the prevailing belief of the soul.

Those who in earth-life have deliberately brought themselves to the con-viction that there is no "hereafter" for the soul, have a peculiar experience. They meet with their kind on a plane in which they imagine that they have been transplanted to another planet and are still in the flesh. And there they are made participants in a great drama of Karma, being made to suffer for the miseries which they have wrought upon others, and to enjoy bless-ings which they have bestowed upon others. They are not punished for the unbelief --- that would be unthinkable injustice --- but they learn the lesson of right and wrong in their own way. This experience, likewise, is purely mental, and arises merely from the expression in Astral manifestation of the memories of their earth-life, urged on by the awakened conscience which gives them "an eye for an eye, and a tooth for a tooth," with a vengeance.

Belief or disbelief in a future state, does not alter the cosmic law of compensation and Astral "purgation." The laws of Karma cannot be defeated by a refusal to believe in a hereafter, nor a refusal to admit the distinction between right and wrong. Every human being has, deep down under the surface though it may be, an intuitive realization of a survival of the soul; and every individual has a deep-seated consciousness of some sort of a moral code. And these subconscious beliefs and opinions come to the surface on the Astral Plane.

Those advanced souls who have given us the best and highest reports of the life of the soul on "the other side," agree in informing us that the highest bliss, and the deepest sorrow, of the disembodied soul of intelligence and culture, comes in the one case from perceiving the effect of -the good actions and thoughts of its earth-life, and, in the other case, from a similar perception of the results of the evil thoughts and actions of its earth life. When the eyes of the soul are cleared so that they may discern the tangled fabric of cause and effect, and follow up each particular thread of its own insertion therein, it has in itself a heaven and a hell of greater intensity than anything of which Dante ever dreamed. There is no joy of the disembodied soul comparable to that experienced from perceiving the logical results of a right action and no sorrow equal to that of perceiving the result of evil action, with its sickening thought of "it might have been otherwise."

But, even these things pass away from the soul. In fact, they often occupy but a moment of time, which seems to the soul as an eternity. There is no such thing as eternal bliss or eternal pain, on the Astral Plane. These things pass away, and the soul emerges once more on earth-life, to once more enroll itself in the School of Life, the Kindergarten of God, there to learn and re-learn its lessons. And remember, always, that both the heaven and the hell of each and every soul, abides in that soul itself. Each soul creates its own heaven and hell --- for neither have any objective existence. The heaven and hell of each soul is the result of its Karma, and is purely a mental creation of its own being. But the phenomena is none the less real to the soul, for this reason. There is nothing in its earthlife which ever seemed more real to it. And again, remember, that heaven and hell, on the Astral Plane, are not given as bribe or punishment, respectively --- but merely as a natural means of developing and unfolding the higher qualities and restraining the lower, to the end that the soul may advance on the Path.

So, once more, we see that in the words quoted at the beginning of this chapter: "Each man is his own absolute law-giver, the dispenser of glory or gloom to himself, the decreer of his own life, his reward, his punishment," on the Astral Plane.

But life on the Astral Plane does not consist entirely of heaven and hell. There are joys experienced which have naught to do with the good or evil deeds of earth-life, but which arise from the urge to express one 's own creative faculties, and to exercise the intellect with increased power --- the joys of expression and knowledge, beyond which mortal cannot hope to experience. In our next chapter we shall consider these phases of life on the Astral Plane.

# CHAPTER XII

## ASTRAL SELF-EXPRESSION

It is one of the saddest features of earth life that we find ourselves unable to express to the fullest the creative impulse, the artistic urge, the striving of the genius within us to unfold itself. After passing a certain place in the scale of life, the evolving soul finds within itself the ever present urge of the something within which is striving to express and unfold itself into objective manifestation. It may be the craving to express in art, music, literature, invention or it may be the insistent desire to be at work remodeling the affairs of the world nearer to the soul's desire. In all of such cases, it is really the creative impulse at work, striving to "make things" in objective form, in accordance with the pattern or model within the soul. And toward such expression, head, heart and hand is eager to work.

But, alas, very few are able to realize in earth-life one tithe of what the soul dreams.

The artistic instinct is ever hungering for perfect expression, and yet it is given but the crumbs that fall from the table. The soul is ever thirsting for progress and achievement, and yet it is given but the few drops that trickle from the fountain. If this one life were all --- if these longings, cravings, desires, and hunger and thirst of the soul, depended only upon the possibilities of the one earth-life --- then indeed would the moaning cry of the pessimists be justified, and the wail of the discouraged be justified. For, in fact, these impulses and cravings are but as the urge of the seed striving to break through its sheaths, that it may put forth stem, branch, blossom and fruit. And the seed can scarce expect to reach the blossom and fruit while it is in the earth.

But, as the advanced occultist knows full well, these seed-desires are but the promise of the future blossom and fruit. The very fact of their existence is a proof of the possibility --- nay, the certainty --- of their fulfillment. So far from being a cause of discouragement, they should be regarded as a prophecy of future achievement and realization. It has been well said that "in every aspiration there dwells the certainty of its own fulfillment." These words seem like mockery to many, and, indeed, they would be mockery were the possibility of realization confined to the one particular earth-life in which they are manifested. But, to the soul which has advanced on the Path of

Attainment sufficiently high that it may look back and down upon the planes of life beneath it, it is seen that these strivings of genius to express itself are but the "labor-pains of the soul," which must precede the future birth of the fruit of genius.

On the Astral Plane these seeds of genius put forth stem and branch, and are prepared for the blossom and fruit of the incarnations ahead of it. In the highly concentrated state of the mind, in certain phases of the Astral life, the talents and genius of the individual grow and develop very rapidly, and the next incarnation finds the individual ready and prepared to manifest the power which he has generated during his sojourn on the Astral. The soul may be said to receive and store up energy while on the Astral, which will enable it to manifest heretofore undreamed of powers in the next earth-life.

A familiar example is that of the boy who is learning to skate, and who finds that he makes little progress during the afternoon. He goes to sleep that night, and forgets all about the art of skating, but when he returns to the task the next day, lo! He finds that he has made wonderful progress. The majority of us have had similar experiences regarding our little tasks in life. We find that something happens to us when we are asleep.

The secret of the above-mentioned phenomena is that, during the sleep of the boy, his sub-conscious or instinctive mind rehearses the task until it has accomplished much in the direction of mastering it, and the next day it puts into practice that which it has learned during the night --- but the conscious mind is not aware of the process of learning. There are depths of the mind which take up these tasks of ours, and which while we are asleep and our objective conscious faculties are resting, straighten out the troublesome kinks of performance, and practice the tasks to be performed the coming day.

In the same way, the super-conscious (not the sub-conscious) faculties of the mind of the soul practice and become proficient in the tasks of the next earth-life, as indicated by the urge of desire and the pangs of achievement seeking birth. But, with this difference, the soul is fully conscious of the workings of the super-conscious faculties, and, in fact, experiences the greatest joy in the work of development and achievement. The heaven world of those souls which are possessed of the desire to "do things "--- to create, to perform, to make --- is indeed a realm of bliss. For there the soul finds itself able to manifest the things which were beyond it during the earth-life, and to express itself in a measure almost beyond the fondest dreams and hopes of the soul on earth.

And this expression and manifestation is performed from the very love of the performance --- from the joy of work, the ecstasy of creative achievement --- rather than from the hope of reward. On the Astral Plane, alone, can the soul find the conditions which are pictured in Kipling's lines:

> And only the Master shall praise us,
> And only the Master shall blame,
> And no one shall work for money,
> And no one shall work for fame;
> But each for the joy of the working,
> And each in his separate star,
> Shall draw the Thing as he sees it
> For the God of Things as They are."

The same thing is true of the seeker after knowledge --- the man to whom the exercise of the intellect is the greatest joy. Such a one finds the Books of Knowledge opened for many pages beyond those at which he was compelled to pause in earth-life. The philosopher, the scientist, the metaphysician, the naturalist --- these find full exercise for their faculties on the Astral Plane. The library of the Cosmos --- the laboratories of the universe --- are at their disposal, and they are made welcome there. They find their heart's desire fulfilled in the opportunities afforded them on the Astral Plane. And, they go back to earth-life, when their time comes for reincarnation, with stimulated intellect and increased reasoning power. What they have thus learned appears in the next life as "intuition."

It is a fact well known to the advanced occultist that great inventors, like Edison --- great philosophers like Hegel, or Herbert Spencer --- great scientists like Darwin or Huxley --- who seemingly manifest intuitive knowledge of their subjects, are but manifesting on the material plane that which they have already acquired on the Astral as the fruition of desires and attempts made in previous incarnations. It is the common experience of such geniuses, as related in their memoirs, that the majority of their greatest discoveries have come to them suddenly as if from a clear sky. But it is a rule of Nature that there is no blossom or fruit without the preceding seed --- and this is true on the mental as well as on the physical plane. There is always a "cause" for the "effect," in these cases.

The struggling genius --- nay, more, the one who feels that he or she could be a genius if that which is within could only be expressed --- these souls will have their chance in the Astral, and if the seed be well planted in the rich soil, of the soul, then in the next incarnation will the blossom and fruit appear. We may carry this idea with us, a little more clearly, perhaps, if we will make the following comparison:

I. The earth-life is like the phase of the crawling caterpillar, which feels within itself a something which it cannot express, and which it scarcely understands;

II. The astral-life is like the phase of the chrysalis, in which the future gorgeous butterfly is being formed, and in which the colored wings already exist in Astral form;

III.    The reincarnated earth-life is like the phase of the butterfly, in which the ideal felt in the first stage and mentally experienced in the second stage becomes fully manifest and active.

The Law of Karma performs much of its work on the Astral Plane, for there the sole material is plastic and non-resistant, the coarse sheaths of the body being absent. And this law is exact and unfailing in its operations --- it always brings the seed to fruition, and each seed brings forth only its own appropriate fruit:

> "Karma --- all that total of a soul
> Which is the thing it did, the thoughts it had,
> The 'self' it wove with woof of viewless time
> Crossed on the warp invisible of acts.
>
> Before beginning, and without an end,
> As space eternal and as surety sure,
> Is fixed a Power divine which moves to good,
> Only its laws endure
>
> That which ye sow, ye reap. See yonder fields
> The sesamum was sesamum, the corn
> Was corn. The silence and the darkness knew;
> So is a man's fate born.

He cometh, reaper of the things he sowed,
Sesamum, corn, so much cast in past birth;
And so much weed and poison stuff, which mar
Him and the aching earth.

If he labor rightly, rooting these,
And planting wholesome seedlings where they grew,
Fruitful and fair and clean the ground shall be,
And rich the harvest due."

# CHAPTER XIII

## ASTRAL PLANE OCCUPATION

Regarding the question of occupation in the heaven-world --- the Astral Plane --- the following from a well-known writer on the subject, Mr. A. P. Sinnett, will prove interesting and instructive:

"Readers, however, who may grant that a purview of earthly life from heaven would render happiness in heaven impossible, may still doubt whether true happiness is possible in the state of monotonous isolation now described. The objection is merely raised from the point of view of an imagination that cannot escape from its present surroundings. To begin with, about monotony. No one will complain of having experienced monotony during the minute, or moment, or half-hour, as it may have been, of the greatest happiness he may have enjoyed in life. Most people have had some happy moments, at all events, to look back to for the purpose of this comparison; and let us take even one such minute or moment, too short to be open to the least suspicion of monotony, and imagine its sensations immensely prolonged without any external events in progress to mark the lapse of time. There is no room, in such a condition of things, for the conception of weariness. The unalloyed, unchangeable sensation of intense happiness goes on and on, not forever, because the causes which have produced it are not infinite themselves, but for very long periods of time, until the efficient impulse has exhausted itself."

Another high authority on the subject (quoted by Sinnett) says: "The moral and spiritual qualities have to find a field in which their energies can expand themselves. Devachan (the higher Astral Plane) is such a field. Hence, all the great planes of moral reform, of intellectual research into abstract principles of Nature --- all the divine, spiritual, aspirations that so fill the brightest part of life, in Devachan come to fruition; and the abstract entity occupies itself in this inner world, also of its own preparation, in enjoying the effects of the grand beneficial spiritual causes sown in life. It lives a purely and spiritually conscious existence --- a dream of realistic vividness --- until Karma, being satisfied in that direction . . . the being moves into its next era of causes, either in this same world or another, according to its stage of progression.

. . . Therefore, there is a 'change of occupation,' a continual change, in Devachan. For that dream-life is but the fruition, the harvest-time, of those

55

psychic germs dropped from the tree of physical existence in our moments of dream and hope --- fancy glimpses of bliss and happiness, stifled in an ungrateful social soil, blooming in the rosy dawn of Devachan, and ripening under its ever-fructifying sky. If man had but a single moment of ideal experience, not even then could it be, as erroneously supposed, the indefinite prolongation of that `single moment.' That one note struck from the lyre of life, would form the key-note of the being's subjective state, and work out into numberless harmonic tones and semi-tones of psychic phantasmagoria. There all unrealized hopes, aspirations and dreams, become fully realized, and the dreams of the objective become the realities of the subjective existence. And there, beyond the curtain of Maya, its vaporous and deceptive appearances are perceived by the Initiate, who has learned the great secret how to penetrate thus deep into the Arcana of Being."

The same authority continues: "To object to this on the ground that one is thus `cheated by Nature,' and to call it 'a delusive sensation of enjoyment which 'has no reality' is to show oneself utterly unfit to comprehend the conditions of life and being outside of our material existence. For how can the same distinction be made in Devachan --- i. e. outside of the conditions of earth-life --- between what we call a reality, and a fictitious or an artificial counterfeit of the same, in this, our world. The same principle cannot apply to the two sets of conditions. ' The spiritual soul has no substance * nor is it confined to one place with a limited horizon of perceptions around it. Therefore, whether in or out of its mortal body, it is ever distinct, and free from its limitations; and, if we call its Devanchanic experiences a cheating of nature,' then we should never be allowed to call 'reality' any of those purely abstract feelings that belong entirely to, and are reflected and assimilated by, our higher soul --- such, for instance, as an ideal perception of the beautiful, profound philanthropy, love, etc, as well as every other purely spiritual sensation that during life fills our inner being with either immense pain or joy." Surely to the aspiring soul there is a far greater happiness in the thought of a heaven-world in which shall be worked out the problems of this life----in which the creative impulse shall be given full opportunity for unfoldment and development, to the end that in a newer and fuller life to come there shall be a putting forth of Blossom and fruit, of heart's desires come true, of ideals made real---than in heaven of the cessation of unfoldment and creative endeavor, where all is finished, where there is nothing to be done or created, where there is no occupation but to fold hands and enjoy the bliss of eternal idleness. The creative instinct is from the very heart of Nature herself, the throbbing of her own life - blood, for nature is ever at work, creating, doing, performing, becoming, making, achieving,---forever, and ever, and ever, on, and on without ceasing, rising from greater to greater achievement, as the aeons of time fly by. Verily this alone is life, and:

"All other life is living death, a land where none but phantoms dwell;
"A wind, a sound, a breath, a voice; the tinkling of the Camel's bell."

And yet so grounded in materiality is the world of men, that they would speak of the heaven-world of the higher Astral Plane as a mirage, a mere dream, a phantasm. They consider nothing "real" unless it is on the material plane. Poor mortals, they do not realize that, at the last, there can be nothing more unreal, more dreamlike, more transitory, more phantasmal, than this very world of material substance. They are not aware that in it there is absolutely no permanence that the mind itself is not quick enough to catch a glimpse of material reality, for, before the mind can grasp a material fact, the fact has merged into something else.

The world of mind, and still, more true, the world of spirit, is far more real than is the world of materiality. From the spiritual viewpoint there is nothing at all real but Spirit; and matter is regarded as the most fleeting and unreal of all illusory appearances. From the same viewpoint, the higher in the scale one rises above the material plane, the more real becomes the phenomena experienced. Therefore, it follows, that the experiences of the soul on the higher Astral Plane are not only not unreal in nature, but, by comparison, are far more real than the experiences of life on the material plans. As the writers just quoted have well said, Nature is not cheated on the Astral Plane --- but Nature herself manifests with more real effect on that plane than on the material plane. This is a hard saying for the uninitiated --- but the advanced soul becomes more and more convinced of its truth every succeeding hour of its experience.

It is a grievous error to regard the experiences of the soul in the heaven-world as little more than a "playing at reality," as some materialistic critics has termed it. One has but to turn to the experiences even of the earth-life to see that some of the world's best work is performed in the hours other than those employed in the actual fashioning of the things. There are times in the everyday life of the most active workers of the world which may be called "the ideal period" --- that is, the time in which the mind creates and forms that which is afterward manifested in material form. There has never been a building, nor a bridge, nor any other great work of human hands,

57

erected, unless first it has been created in the mind of some man or men. It has had its first existence in the creative faculties of the mind --- the material building is merely the reproduction of the mental creation. This, being remembered, which shall we consider the real creation, the mental or the material?

The soul, in its activities on the higher Astral Plane, performs a work similar to that of the mind of the inventor, designer, builder, when it fashions and designs that which will afterward be objectified in material form. It may be called the period or stage of forming the model, or pattern, or mould, which shall afterward serve for the material manifestation. Ignorance, alone, can conceive of such a stage of existence as being a "mere dream." Verily, the scales of matter serve to blind the eyes of man, so that he sees the real as the unreal --- the unreal as the real. The higher in the scale of existence the soul rises, the more real are its experiences --- the nearer it approaches matter, in its descent of the scale, the more unreal are its experiences. Ah, Maya! Maya! Thou mother of illusion, when shall we learn to rise above thy spell! Those who play in the clay, are besmeared by it, and can see nothing finer and higher than its sticky substance.

# CHAPTER XIV

## ASTRAL COMPANIONSHIP

There is a question which ever comes to the mind of those who indulge in speculations regarding "the other side "--- that question which is voiced in the words of the familiar old hymn: "Shall we know each other there?" This query is rooted in the very heart of human love and affection. Heaven, even if it furnished every other joy and satisfaction, would not be heaven to the average person if it did not also furnish companionship and association with those loved in earth life. The soul instinctively craves for the society not only of those close to it by ties of the love of man and woman, but also of those to which it is bound by the relationship of parent and child; brother and sister; friend and friend. Without this assurance of continued companionship and association, heaven would seem a very bleak and cold place to the average human soul.

We are glad that the Yogi teachers have been very explicit and plain upon this subject, and that their students may find that this hope and desire of the human heart has a full and rich realization in the facts of life on the Astral Plane. Not only do we "know each other there," but we are naturally bound by Astral bonds of attraction to those whom we love and to those with whom we are in sympathy, even though we had never known them in earth life. More than this, there is, on the Astral Plane, the possibility of a far nearer and closer companionship between kindred souls than earth-life ordinarily witnesses. With the dropping and discarding of the sheaths of the physical body, the soul becomes capable of a far closer relation to kindred souls than it ever experienced on the physical plane. The Astral fires having burnt up the dross of the lower attractions, the soul is able to function on much higher planes of association. On the Astral Plane, soul may meet soul in close communion and comradeship and the dreams and longings of earth-life, which were found impossible of realization on that plane, now become the ordinary incidents of the new life of the soul. That for which the soul has longed for in vain on earth, now is found in its richest fruition.

To realize just what this means, it is necessary but to think of the highest ideals entertained by the soul, in earth-life, regarding the relationships between human beings. Though these ideals are seldom lived up to in earth life, nevertheless they abide with the soul constantly, and it is one of the tragedies of earth life that these ideals always seem "too good to be true."

The love of man and woman, of the right kind, always has as its background this ideal affection and desire, and yet how seldom does the ideal escape being dragged in the mud. The relationship between parent and child, between brothers and sisters, between friends, seldom is found to approach the ideal which dwells ever in the human heart. So true is this ideal --- so constant is its presence --- that when, in earth-life, we see a companionship which seems even partially to comply with the ideal requirements, our deepest feelings are touched. In fiction, in poetry, in song, in the drama, we find that the picture of the realization of this ideal touches springs of emotion and sympathy which lift us up to higher planes of thought and life. What then must be the joy, the bliss, the happiness, the satisfaction, of a life on a plane of being in which this expression is the only natural one, and where the ideal becomes the real is actual expression?

Yes, we do, indeed, "know each other there." Not only the "other" whom we may have in mind, but also many "others" with whom we are in natural soul harmony. Those who are bound together by the bond of earth love, relationship, and friendship --- providing that there really is a bond of attachment of any degree between them --- have full opportunity to manifest their mutual affection and harmonic attraction on the higher Astral Plane. The highest that the human imagination can picture as possible in such companionship, is but as a faint shadow to the actual reality of the experience. It is useless to attempt to paint a picture of these scenes and relationships, for there are no words with which to express the truth. The answer to the inquiry must necessarily be: that each soul that asks the question turn its mental gaze inward, and find the picture, painted in the imagination, of the highest possible bliss that would be possible in such a state and condition, and then consider that even this imaginary picture falls a thousand times short of the reality.

It is only in the harmony of music, or the rhythmic cadences of the best poetry, or the lines of some great work of art, that the earth dwelling soul may catch a glimpse of the truth of Love on the higher Astral Plane. These things at times cause to rise in the soul faint hints of what the soul actually experiences on those higher planes of being. This is one of the reasons why music, art, and poetry are able at times to lift us above the material environment in which we are dwelling. In the flashes of Cosmic Conscience which occasionally come to souls of spiritual enlightenment, there is included a realization of this feature of the association of souls on the higher planes. Well has the Western poet expressed the difficulty of stating, in ordinary words, the truth of this realization of the truth --- in broken measures and stammering tongue:

"As in a swoon, one instant,
Another sun, ineffable, full dazzles me,
And all the orbs I knew, and brighter, unknown orbs,
One instant of the future land, Heaven's land.

I cannot be awake, for nothing looks to me
as it did before,
Or else I am awake for the first time,
and all before has been a mean sleep.
When I try to tell the best I find, I cannot;
My tongue is ineffectual, on its pivots,
My breath will not be obedient to its organs,
I become a dumb man." ---Whitman.

"Words from a man who speaks from that life must sound vain to those who do not dwell in the same thought on their own part. I dare not speak for it. My words do not carry its august sense; they fall short and cold. Only itself can inspire whom it will, and behold! Their speech shall be lyrical, and sweet, and universal as the rising of the wind. Yet I desire, even by profane words, if sacred I may not use, to indicate the heaven of this deity, and to report what hints I have collected of the transcendent simplicity and energy of the Highest Law." --- Emerson.

The difficulty in explaining to the earth dweller the nature and character of the companionship of the higher planes of the Astral, is that his mind insists upon thinking in terms of place, whereas there is no "place" on the Astral --- merely conditions and states, as we have explained. To dwell in the "same place" as the loved one, on the Astral Plane, means simply to dwell in the same state or condition of being, and thus be brought into a closer relation- ship, a greater degree of nearness, than nearness in space can furnish. There is a greater "in touchness' by reason of this harmony of Astral condition than the earth-dweller can imagine. Only the advanced soul can begin to compre- hend this mystery of Astral Life. It can be pictured only faintly by reference to the state of soulful "oneness" experienced at times by lovers, when it seems as if the limitations of the flesh have been transcended, and the two souls have blended into one. This is far more than mere nearness in space or place --- and yet even this but faintly indicates the ideal condition of the Astral Life.

It may be questioned by some, how souls enjoying this companionship, if they happen to dwell on different planes of Astral being, can be in the same state or condition in which the experience is rendered possible. The answer is simple to one who is familiar with the highest occult truths. It is this: the soul on the higher planes feels the sympathetic attraction of the soul on the lower plane, and, answering it, establishes a psychic connection (akin to a highly exalted form of telepathy) between the two, and thus renders possible the experience of the closest mental and spiritual relationship and companionship, which experience far transcends the companionship of two souls in the flesh. Moreover, as we have explained in a previous chapter, the soul on the higher plane may actually visit, with all of its soul-being, another soul on a plane lower than itself. In this, and other ways, companionship between disembodied souls of the Astral Plane is manifested. There is no "lonesomeness," or loneliness for souls who crave sympathy on the Astral. There is nothing that is high, and ennobling, in earth-life, that has not its magnified correspondence on the Astral Plane --- only the dross being left behind.

There is a natural law which operates on the Astral Plane, as well as upon the material plane, and this law regulates and controls everything on that plane. The disembodied soul does not part with Nature, when it leaves the earth-life--but, rather it rises to a plane of Nature which is fuller, richer, and sweeter in every way than the best of which the earth dwelling soul dreams. The dross of materiality burned away by the Astral vibrations, the soul blossoms and bears spiritual fruit in the new life. There is one word, which, above all others, expresses the spirit-meaning, and purpose of the higher planes --- and the phenomena thereof --- that word is LOVE! And that Love is the "Perfect Love which casteth out all Fear "--- and its blossom is Joy --- and its fruit is Peace!

# CHAPTER XV

## "SPIRIT COMMUNICATION"

To the mind of the advanced occultist there are few things more deplorable than the confusion; half-truths commingled with untruth; false doctrine; false conclusions; some concerned with the subject of "spirit communication" in the mind of the Western world. And yet, this confusion, as deplorable as it may be, has served, nevertheless, to attract the attention of thinking people to the subject, and to lead them to further investigation of the matter. Even the fraudulent practices which have been such a scandal in the history of spiritualism in the Western world, as disgusting and revolting as they have been to the mind of thoughtful persons, have served to bring into relief the real truth behind the general phenomena of spiritualism. Leaving entirely out of consideration the fraudulent, and semi-fraudulent, phenomena which masquerades as "spirit communication," the subject of the communication between persons in the flesh and souls out of the flesh may be divided into two general classes, i. e. the lower and the higher, respectively. The lower class is composed of (1) cases in which disembodied souls, of a low order --- the so-called "earth-bound" souls --- manifest their presence to persons still in the flesh; or (2) cases of the animation of "Astral shells." The higher class of the phenomena of "spirit communication," so called, consists of cases in which the souls on the higher planes of the Astral manifest their presence to persons in the flesh.

The soul on the higher Astral planes, dwells in the idealistic condition, concerning itself not with the affairs of the world it has left behind it. It, of course, maintains a sympathetic connection with those near and dear to it by ties of love or friendship who have been left behind on the material plane, but such sympathetic connection is entirely of a psychic or spiritual nature, and has no connections with nearness in space, or physical proximity. The ties and bonds between the disembodied soul and the soul still in the flesh in earth-life may be thought of as spiritual filaments --- something like a transcendent form of telepathic rapport. When the disembodied soul is thinking of the loved one on earth, the latter frequently experiences a feeling akin to the physical nearness of the disembodied soul, but this merely arises from the sensing of the mental and spiritual rapport of which we have just spoken. In the same way, the disembodied soul experiences a sense of "call" or message from the person in the flesh when the latter is thinking intently of the former.

So far as this continuance of the feelings of love and affection between the separated souls is concerned, nothing but good can be said, for the soul in the flesh is comforted and strengthened by the feeling of rapport and nearness of the disembodied soul on the Astral Plane and the disembodied soul experiences pleasure and joy just as it would on earth-life by the physical nearness of the loved one. This relationship is a peculiarly sacred one, and is enjoyed by many persons in the flesh, although they may have but little to say regarding it to others who would not understand. Those who have had this experience will recognize just what is meant by these words, when they read them. Others, who have not had these experiences, can understand them only by reference to the greatest feeling of soul-nearness they ever have experienced in earth-life. It is, indeed, a communion of soul with soul, almost approaching the perfection of soul-communion on the Astral Plane in some of its aspects, although always leaving a something lacking from the very nature of the case. We wish to be distinctly understood as having nothing but good to say regarding this form of "spirit-communication" between persons bound by ties of love and friendship, one out of the flesh and the other still in earth life. What we shall now proceed to condemn, is something of an entirely different nature.

Advanced occultists are practically unanimously agreed that the practice of recalling the attention of disembodied spirits for mere entertainment, curiosity, or general "exhibition" purposes is most deplorable. The best authorities condemn the practice in the strongest terms. In the first place, the result is always unsatisfactory, for very good and sufficient occult reasons. In the second place, the effect of such recalling is apt to be detrimental to the disembodied soul, by reason of withdrawing its spiritual attention from the things of the higher planes, and turning them back to the things of the material plane, thus retarding its development and unfoldment, and also confusing its mind. It is akin to directing the mind of the growing child back to the things of its prenatal condition, if such a thing were possible. And, to the soul which does not understand the nature and character of its Astral Life (and none but the most advanced souls so do understand) the mixing of the things and phenomena of the material and Astral Planes is most perplexing, confusing, and distracting. The soul should be left to unfold naturally on its new plane, and not called back to earth to satisfy curiosity or to furnish entertainment. The result arising from the latter course is akin to that which would arise were one to persist in pulling up a plant each day to see whether its roots were sprouting and growing.

Another form of recalling the disembodied soul --- that of calling it back to comfort and inform loving friends and relatives --- is scarcely less undesirable. The disembodied soul, drawn back by the pull upon its sympathetic bonds of connection, comes back like a person walking in his sleep, for such is almost precisely its condition. Sleep walking is not a desirable thing to induce in persons on earth, and is no better when it is induced in a disembodied soul. It comes from its Astral experiences in a dazed condition, and gives but little satisfaction to those recalling it, and really suffers a confusing and perplexing experience itself. Those who have had experiences with the recalling of disembodied souls (where the phenomena is genuine) will readily remember the dazed and generally confused answers given, and the generally unsatisfactory results obtained even under the best conditions. The practice of recalling souls from the Astral Plane is a clear perversion of Nature's processes, and the result is never satisfactory. This practice is never justified, and the best authorities severely condemn it. The glimpse into the nature and condition of the Astral Plane life, which we have given you in this book, should be sufficient for you to see clearly the reason of this opinion, and the cause of the condemnation.

It is true that souls on the Astral Plane, sometimes, under stress of strong memories or worries regarding those they have left behind, have returned voluntarily to the plane of earth-life, and have made themselves known to persons dwelling thereon --- even to the extent of actual materialization, at times. These cases are unusual, but are sufficiently frequent to be noted in this connection. In such cases, the strength of the desire of the disembodied soul has caused it to take on objective form to the senses of those to whom it appears, just as a very strong telepathic impression will take on objective form. But, even in such cases, the poor worried soul gradually passes beyond the attraction of earth-life, and ceases to return to its former scenes, but begins to live out its normal Astral Life in accordance with Nature's laws and plans.

We know that in uttering these truths we are bringing disappointment, and possibly resentment, to the minds of some in earth-life who are fond of the thought that they are in frequent communication with the souls of their departed friends and loved ones. But the truth is the truth, and we are assured that a proper understanding of the subject will reveal to such persons that the highest love for those who have gone before will consist in doing that which is best for those loved ones, so that they will not persist in sacrificing this best interest for the selfish purpose of temporary satisfaction on their own part. Nay, more, the "satisfaction" is never really satisfying --- there is always the consciousness that there is something missing, something lacking.

True love consists in giving, rather than in getting. And, is not this true in the matter of communication with those loved ones on "the other side?" Is it not a higher and nobler thing to send them loving thoughts and sympathy, cheering and encouraging them in the unfoldment on the higher planes, than to endeavor to drag them back to the lower plane of materiality for the sake of hearing them say that they are happy and that all is all right with them, and, perhaps, to mumble some semi-coherent platitudes in the manner of a somnambulist? And is it not more worthy of ourselves, who are dwelling in the bonds of the flesh, to raise the plane of our communion with those on the other side to their own higher plane of being, and to commune with them along the lines of spiritual understanding and rapport --- in the silence and without spoken words --- on the plane where soul may speak to soul without the medium of words, and without the necessity of physical presence? Think over these things, and let your soul speak the truth to you from its inmost heart --- be assured that the answer will be one with the truths of the highest authorities.

# CHAPTER XVI

## EARTH BOUND SOULS

In the works upon the subject of the Astral Plane, particularly if the work be by one of the old authorities, there will be found many references to what are called "earth-bound" souls. As a rule, these references are to the lower order of souls, which refuse to lift their mental gaze beyond the things and scenes of earth, and which haunt their old scenes of activity and life, finding therein the only pleasure that is possible to them in their degraded condition. But, in this consideration, we must not neglect a mention of a higher order of souls who, unfortunately, are slow to break their earthly bonds, and who cling closely to those who have been left behind them. Let us consider this last class for a moment.

It sometimes happens that a soul who is naturally fitted for the normal life on the higher Astral Planes, is so tied and attached to matters concerning earth-life, that after its awakening from the soul-slumber it at first refuses to participate in the normal Astral existence, but, instead, busies itself with the affairs of earth-life which it should have left behind it. This unfortunate condition arises generally from some sense of unperformed duty, remorse, or anxiety about the welfare of some loved one left behind. In such cases it actually hovers in space around the presence of the person or place in which it is interested, and, under extraordinary psychic conditions it may actually make itself visible to the senses of persons in the flesh.

To this class belong the poor afflicted souls which wander about, haunting the scene of their earthly misdeeds, their remorse causing them to make vain endeavors to undo or atone for their misdeeds. Of course, these unfortunate souls are not fully "wide-awake" on the Astral Plane, neither are they wide awake on the earth-life plane. Instead, they act like somnambulists, on either plane, failing to partake of the normal life of either phase of existence. Akin to these are those worried and tormented souls who feel that they have left some duty or task unfulfilled, and who in a somnambulistic condition hover around their former scenes of life, endeavoring dreamily to set matters right. A third class is composed of a few who are so attached personally to souls left behind in the flesh, that they brood over the loved persons, impotently striving to aid and guide them.

In all of these cases, there is but one duty for those in the flesh to perform

--- and that duty is plainly marked. This duty consists in mentally advising the poor souls that their proper scene of activity is on the Astral Plane; that their duty demands that they cease brooding and hovering over earth scenes and that they yield themselves to the upward attraction, rise to their proper plane of Astral existence, and enjoy the blessings thereof. Those who are conscious of the presence of disembodied souls of this type should not shrink from this duty, no matter how much it may pain them to instruct the disembodied soul in this way. It is like talking to a young child, in the majority of cases, (owing to the semi-sleep condition of the earth-bound soul of this type). Although the soul may grieve and weep like a child, like the child it should be bidden to do its duty and to go to its spiritual abode. This advice will often be heeded by the earthbound soul, and it will yield to the upward attraction, and cease its troubled existence. However, in time, even without such advice, the attraction of the higher spheres will prevail, and the soul will rise to its rightful place on the Astral. We caution everyone against encouraging the earth-bound soul to remain. It is like encouraging the un-born child to remain in the womb, or the unfolding butterfly to remain in the chrysalis stage. No good comes from encouraging a violation of Nature's laws, on any plane of existence, including the Astral.

The lower class of earth-bound souls belong to an entirely different category from those just mentioned. This lower class is composed of souls of a very low degree of spiritual development --- those in which animality is predominant, and brutish materiality the characteristic emotional attribute. These souls are considered as "earthbound" by reason of the fact that the attraction of the material earth-plane so overbalances the urge of the upward attraction that the latter is more than neutralized, and the soul lives on a plane as near the material plane as is possible to it. In fact, the lower planes of the Astral inhabited by this class of souls is so little removed from the material plane that it may be spoken of as almost a transition stage between the material and the astral plane --- a blending of the two. It is as if a very thin veil were placed between this plane and the scenes of material life --- a tantalizingly thin veil it is to these low souls --- so that while these souls may not actually participate in the earthly affairs, they may yet be dimly conscious of them.

These low earth-bound souls, as a rule confine their earth visitations and brooding to the actual scenes which have attracted them in earth-life. And these souls take a fiendish delight in trying to influence those of their own kind still in the flesh, when in a muddled condition, urging them to fresh infamies and often to actual crimes. In some extreme case's these low souls have been known actually to seek their own discarded Astral shell, or even that of another of their kind, and by a great effort cause it to materialize for a short time in objective form as a "ghost." The nature of these entities changes but little by their transition to the Astral, and they take the same delight in "rough-house" performances, practical jokes, etc., as in their days in the flesh. Many instances of ghostly appearances, the throwing about of physical objects, etc., have been due to this class of disembodied earthbound souls. They always may be dismissed and caused to disappear by the person in the flesh showing them that he understands their real nature, and bidding them begone. A bold front, and authoritative command, coupled with words showing that their pretenses are "seen through" will always rout these creatures, and send them back where they belong, crestfallen and abashed.

Another favorite amusement of a certain class of this kind of low disembodied souls, is that of appearing in Astral form, by taking advantage of an Astral shell, in spiritualistic seances, or other gatherings in which the psychic conditions are so sufficiently strong and favorable as to aid in the materialization. In such cases these creatures often impudently strive to impersonate other souls, either of some friend or relative of some one present, or else of some historical character. Anyone who has ever attended spiritualistic seances and seen "George Washington," or "Julius Caesar" appear and converse in the tone and words of the Bowery, of White chapel, will readily understand the reason thereof. A knowledge of this fact will serve to throw light on many perplexing phases of psychic phenomena.

These lower class souls, however, spend but a short term on the Astral Plane, and very soon pass on to reincarnation in surroundings corresponding with their natures, and to which they are attracted by spiritual laws. Their whole attraction being toward the physical and the material, there is nothing to hold them on the Astral Plane, and their abode there is of very brief duration, in the majority of cases. And, yet, even in the very worst and most brutal person, there is always a little of the good, and a spark of spiritual glow, which brightens a little during each visit to the Astral Plane. And, in the course of time, this little spark is sufficiently kindled to manifest a tiny blaze, which Heats the way of the poor soul and illumines the road toward higher things. So that even among these poor entities there is at least a certain degree of hope and promise. But the majority are degenerated and fallen souls --- descended from a once higher state --- who, if they fail to profit by the pains of the material life, are apt to tend still further downward until kind Nature wipes them out as independent entities, and resolves them back to

69

their original spiritual elements.

There are sub-planes of the Astral so low and degraded that we hesitate to mention them. They are inhabited by the very lowest and most degraded and degenerate souls --- souls which are on the sure descent to annihilation, being unfit to serve as carriers of the sacred plane. Of the details of these sub plans, we shall not speak at this place. Enough to quote the words of two distinguished occultists, one of a former age, and one of to-day. The old sage said of these sub-planes: "What manner of place is this I see. It hath no water. It hath no air. It bath no light. It hath no foundation. It is unfathomably deep. It is as black as the blackest night." The latter-day investigator says: "Most students find the investigation of this section an extremely unpleasant task for there appears to be a sense of density and gross materiality about it which is indescribably loathsome to the liberated Astral body, causing the sense of pushing its way through some black viscous fluid, while the inhabitants and influences there are unusually undesirable."

It should scarcely be necessary to warn persons not to dabble in psychic phenomena of a material character, which brings them more or less into contact with these lower planes of the Astral. But, nevertheless, we do wish to set forth this warning in this place, just as we have elsewhere in our works. For there is always the temptation and fascination of the unknown for many persons, usually those who are not familiar with the phenomena of the Astral Plane. Such persons, like "fools, rush in where angels fear to tread," and attract to themselves all sorts of undesirable Astral entities and conditions. Our general advice on this subject is: keep the mind fixed on the higher truths of the spirit, and the higher life of the soul; and turn the face resolutely away from the lower forms of psychic phenomena; in fact, do not seek "phenomena" at all, but seek ever the Truth which, when known, makes all other things clear. Seek ever the sunshine of Spirit, and avoid the baleful glare of the psychic moon.

# CHAPTER XVII

## ASTRAL SHELLS

We would be neglecting the task to which we have set ourselves in this book, were we to omit all mention of a peculiar phenomenon of the Astral Plane which causes much confusion to all beginners in the investigation of psychic phenomena. We allude to what have aptly been called "Astral Shells," the worn out Astral bodies of the souls who have awakened from the soul-slumber of the Astral Plane. These worn-out garments of the soul are frequently mistaken for the soul itself, and much confusion has arisen by reason of this mistake.

Each human entity on earth-life has, in addition to the physical body, a finer and more subtle form of body, which is called the Astral Body (sometimes called "the etheric double," known to the Hindus as the Linga Sharira). This Astral body is an exact counterpart of the physical body, and, in fact, is the finer model upon which the physical body is moulded or overlaid. Upon the departure of the soul from the physical body, it carries the Astral body with it as its vehicle, and dwells in it during the soul-sleep, discarding it only when it awakens from the soul-slumber and passes on to the higher states or conditions of the Astral. The Astral body, thus discarded by the soul, then becomes what is known to occultists as an "Astral shell."

In a previous work, we have spoken as follows of the "Astral shell," after it has been discarded by the soul: "The Astral body exists for some time after the death of the person to whom it belongs, and under certain circumstances, it is visible to living persons, and is by them called a 'ghost.' The "Astral shell," which is sometimes seen after it has been sloughed off by the soul which has passed on, is in such cases nothing more than a corpse of finer matter than its physical counterpart. In such cases it is possessed of no life or intelligence, and is nothing more than a cloud seen in the sky bearing a resemblance to the human form. It is a shell, nothing more. . . . When discarded by the soul it begins to slowly disintegrate. . . It floats around in the lower Astral atmosphere, until finally it is dissolved into its original elements. It seems to have a peculiar attraction toward its late physical counterpart, and will often return to the neighborhood of the discarded physical body, and disintegrate with it. Persons of psychic sight, either normal or influenced by fear or similar emotions, frequently see these "Astral shells" floating around graveyards, over battle-fields, etc., and mistake them for the 'spirits' of departed persons, whereas they are no more the real souls of the persons than are the physical bodies beneath the ground."

"These 'Astral shells' may be 'galvanized' into a semblance of life by coming in contact with the vitality of some 'medium,' the prana of the latter animating it, and the sub-conscious mentality of the medium causing it to manifest signs of life and partial intelligence. At Some of the seances of the mediums, these astral shells are materialized by means of the vitality of the medium, and are made to talk in a stupid, disconnected way with those around, but it is not the person himself talking, but a mere shell animated by the life principle of the medium and the 'circle,' and acting and talking like an automaton. There are, of course, other forms of 'spirit return,' but investigators of spiritualistic phenomena should beware of confounding these 'Astral shells' with the real soul of their departed friends."

A leading authority on the subject has written of the "Astral shell," as follows: "At death it is disembodied for a brief period, and, under some abnormal conditions, may even be temporarily visible to the external sight of still living persons. Under such conditions it is taken of course for the ghost of the departed persons. Spectral apparitions may sometimes be occasioned in other ways, but the third principle (the Astral Body) when that results in a visible phenomenon, is a mere aggregation of molecules in a peculiar state, having no life or consciousness of any kind whatever. It is no more than a cloud-wreath in the sky which happens to settle into the semblance of some animal form. Broadly speaking, the linga sharira never leaves the body except at death, case. When seen at all, and this can but nor migrates far from the body even in that rarely occur, it can only be seen near where the physical body lies. it . . It is a mistake to speak of consciousness, as we understand the feeling in life, attaching to the 'Astral shell' or remnant but, nevertheless, a certain spurious resemblance may be awakened in that shell, and without baying any connection with the real consciousness all the while growing in strength and vitality in the spiritual sphere. There is no power on the part of the shell of taking on and assimilating new ideas and initiating courses of action on the basis of those new ideas. But there is in the shell a survival of volitional impulses imparted to it during life. . . . It is liable to be galvanized for a time in the mediumistic current into a state of consciousness and life which may be suggested by the first condition of a person who, carried into a strange room in a state of insensibility during illness, wakes up feeble, confused in mind, gazing about with a blank feeling of bewilderment, taking in impressions, hearing words addressed to him and answering vaguely. Such a state of consciousness is unassociated with the notions of past and future. It is an automatic consciousness, derived from the medium."

Another writer on the subject says of these "Astral shells:" "These remnants of the Astral bodies so discarded and disintegrating are not in any way related to the souls which formerly inhabited them. They are mere shells, without soul or mind, and yet preserving a slight degree of vitality. They are Astral corpses, just as much a corpse as is the discarded physical body. But, just as the physical corpse may be aroused into apparent life activity by a strong galvanic current, and will roll its eyes, move its limbs, and even utter groans --- so may these Astral corpses be galvanized by the vitality of a medium (unconsciously by the latter), if the conditions be favorable, and may be materialized so as to appear as a shadowy form, acting, moving, and even speaking, the only mind in it, however, being supplied by that of the medium or the persons present at the seance."

The careful student of occultism will find in the works of all of the best authorities many warnings against the confounding of the phenomena related to these "Astral shells," with that referring to actual communication between disembodied souls and those in the flesh. But the general public, not being informed, is very apt to fall into the error of supposing that this class of psychic phenomena is a manifestation of "spirit return," and the cause of rational spiritualism has been very much injured in this way. It is a ghastly mockery to have these disintegrating "Astral shells," galvanized temporarily into life by the vitality and minds of a medium (consciously or otherwise), and to have them mistaken for the souls of departed friends and relatives. And yet this terrible experience has been the lot of many earnest investigators of psychic phenomena, and by many persons whose love has prompted them to seek to communicate once more with their loved ones. It would seem that there is much need for true occult knowledge on the part of the public, in these days when so many are dabbling in psychic research, and producing psychic phenomena the nature and character of which they do not understand.

We trust that nothing we have said in this, or the preceding chapters, will be taken as an attack upon modern spiritualism in the Western world. We have no such intention, and no such feeling. We realize that through the channel of modern spiritualism many earnest souls have been brought to a realization of the higher spiritual truths, and have been led to the door of the higher occult understanding. In fact, modern spiritualism to-day is concerning itself

73

comparatively little with "phenomena," but, instead, is striving to unfold the truths of the life on the higher spheres of being and existence of the soul. But following on the outskirts of the movement are many to whom only phenomena of the most sensational character appeals --- it is for these that this warning is intended. And, in the same manner, for those who are following idly after the "psychic research" movement, being attracted thereto by love of novelty and hope of excitement. We would warn both of these classes of investigators that in opening the doors of the minds and souls to lower Astral influences, they are running great risks. There are swamps and quagmires of the Astral world into which the unwary feet are apt to sink. Therefore we say

## "BEWARE OF THE LOWER ASTRAL

VIBRATIONS." Keep the mind and soul centered on the higher truths, and resist the temptation to dabble in the phenomena of the lower states. There is no satisfaction in the Moon phase of occultism, and great dangers are often encountered --- turn your face toward the SUN! Live on the spiritual Heights --- beware of the miasmatic swamps and malarial quagmires on the lowlands of psychism. These warnings cannot be too often repeated by those having the interest of the race at heart.

# CHAPTER XVIII

## THE SECOND SOUL-SLEEP

One of the many facts which are impressed upon the minds of the student of the occult is that which illustrates the principle that Nature is consistent and uniform in her methods. On the various planes of being, Nature has a few fundamental methods or habits of manifestation which the student soon learns to look for in his investigations, and which he always finds if he continues his search sufficiently long and with sufficient care and watchfulness.

One of these constant methods of habits of Nature is that by which she always interposes a period of rest, pause, sleep, or recuperation between the end of one period of activity and the beginning of another. On the physical plane we have many instances of this, from the momentary pause of the pendulum between its forward and backward swing; the pause between the inhalation and exhalation of the breath; the sleep between the close of one day and the beginning of another; the period of rest of the unborn child between its formative period and its birth into the world, etc.

In the Astral world we find the same phenomenon in the soul-slumber which occurs between that which we call Death and the beginning of the new existence on the Astral Plane. And, reasoning from analogy, we might naturally expect to be informed that a similar phase or period exists between the close of the activities of the soul on the Astral Plane and its passing on to reincarnation or to higher spheres of spiritual life. And, indeed, such a phase or period does exist, and forms a very distinct feature of the soul's existence on "the other side." Such phase or period is known to occultists as the "second soul-sleep," or slumber.

The second soul-sleep is preceded by a transition state of gradually declining activity and consciousness, and a corresponding desire for rest on the part of the soul. The natural processes on the Astral Plane nearing their close, the soul begins to experience a feeling of lassitude and weariness, and instinctively longs for rest and repose. It finds that it has lived out the greater part of its desires, ambitions, and ideals, and in many cases has also out-lived them. There comes to it that wistful feeling of having fulfilled the purpose of its destiny, and a premonition of the coming of some newer phase of existence. The soul does not feel pain at the approach of the second soul-sleep, but, on the contrary, experiences satisfaction and happiness as the

75

coming of something which promises rest and recuperation. Like the weary traveler who has climbed the mountain paths, and has delighted in the experiences of the journey, the soul feels that it has well earned a restful repose, and, like that traveler, it looks forward to the same with longing and desire.

The soul may have passed but a few years, or perhaps a hundred or a thousand years, of earth-time, on the Astral Plane, according to its degree of development and unfoldment. But, be its stay short or long, the feeling of weariness reaches it at last, and, like many aged persons in earth-life, it feels that "my work is over --- let me pass on, let me pass on." Sooner or later, the soul feels a desire to gain new experience, and to manifest in a new life some of the advancement which has come to it by reason of its unfoldment on the Astral Plane. And, from these reasons, and also from the attraction of the desires which have been smouldering there, not lived out or cast off or, possibly influenced by the fact that some loved soul, on a lower plane, is ready to incarnate, and wishing to be with that soul (which is also a form of desire) the soul falls into a current sweeping toward rebirth and the selection of proper parents and advantageous circumstances and surroundings. In consequence thereof it again falls into a state of soul-slumber, gradually, and so when its time comes it "dies" on the Astral Plane, as it did before on the material plane, and passes forward toward re-birth on earth.

But, strictly speaking, the soul continues in a condition of partial slumber even after it has been re-born on earth-life, for it does not at once wake up in the body of the newborn child, in which form it has reincarnated. On the contrary, it awakens gradually during the early childhood and youth, of the child. This is a most interesting fact of occult science, and one that is but little known even to many careful students. We have spoken of it as follows, in a previous work: "A soul does not fully awaken from its second soul slumber immediately upon re-birth, but exists in a dream-like state during the days of infancy, its gradual awakening being evidenced by the growing intelligence of the babe, the brain of the child keeping pace with the demands made upon it. In some cases, however, the awakening is premature, and we see cases of prodigies, child-geniuses, etc., but such cases are more or less abnormal and unhealthy. Occasionally, the dreaming soul in the child half-wakes, and startles us by some profound observation, or mature remark or conduct. . . . The rare instances of precocious children and infant genius, are illustrations of cases in which the awakening has been more than ordinarily rapid. On the other hand, cases are known where the soul does not awaken as rapidly as the average, and the result is that the person does not show signs of full intellectual activity until nearly middle-age. Cases are known where men seem to 'wake up' when they are forty years of age, or even older, and then take on freshened activity and energy, surprising those who had known them before."

But we are principally concerned now with the earlier stages of the second soul-slumber --- the stages which are passed on the Astral Plane. In these early stages, the slumbering soul undergoes a peculiar stage of what might be called "spiritual digestion and assimilation." Just as, in its first soul-slumber, the soul digested the fruits of its earth-life and assimilated the lessons and experiences thereof, so in this second slumber the soul digests and assimilates the wonderful experiences of the Astral. For, be it remembered, the period on the Astral has been not only one of retrospect on the one hand, and manifestation of latent powers, on the other. It has also been a period of reconstruction and unfoldment.

Many things have been lived-out and outlived on the Astral, and the soul leaves the Astral a far different entity from that which entered it. But, and remember this also, the change is always for the better. Many undesirable characteristics have been burned away by the fires of repentance and remorse, and many desirable characteristics have been unfolded in the rich spiritual soil of the higher planes, aided by the Sun of Spirit which envelopes the soul on the higher planes. But, there is still needed a process of "stock taking," readjustment of mental conditions, and spiritual preparation for a new life --- and this is supplied during the early stages of the second soul-slumber.

Just as the child, or the adult, receives the energy necessary for the work of the new day, when it is wrapped in sleep at the close of the old day, so does the sleeping soul receive energy from the One Supply, that it may face the new life with vigor and power. We do not go into the details of this recuperative work at this place, as we wish to avoid all appearance of technicality. Enough to say that the soul receives a fresh impetus of energy, and is also given the "psychic pattern" of its new physical body, during the second soul-slumber. It is also allowed to experience the attractive power of its Karmic ties, which leads it into the channel of rebirth in accordance with the character of its nature --- "like attracts like," is the axiom which expresses the processes.

Each soul goes to where it belongs by reason of what it is. It is not subject to the arbitrary dictates of any being in heaven or in earth, but the absolutely just and equitable law of Karma operates in every case. There is no favoritism, nor is there the slightest chance of even the faintest injustice being the fate of any soul, no matter how humble or lowly it may be. The lowest as well as the highest comes under the same law, for all are children of the same parent --- all little children in the kindergarten of the Absolute. All are on The Path, whether they know it or not --- and their ignorance is not counted against them in the reckoning.

In the last chapter of this book, we shall speak of a class of souls that rise above further reincarnation in earth-life, and ascend to planes and stages of existence far above anything which the earth can offer. We mention them here merely to say that even such souls must pass through the second soul-slumber of the Astral Plane before they can proceed further. In such cases they lose in their sleep all that is left of the confining sheaths of earth-desire, and throw aside all the fruits of earth action except that which is called Liberation and Freedom. Such souls never again awaken on earth, nor do they ever return thereto, unless, perchance, they voluntarily revisit earth in after ages as great teachers or leaders. Such have worn the garb of men, now and then throughout the ages, but have always been far more than men in all but form. There are planes upon planes of existence higher than earth or its Astral Plane. Blessed indeed is the soul which awakens from the second soul-slumber and finds itself in even the most humble of these exalted states. Even the wisest sage bows his head in reverence at the mention of such spheres of existence, which transcend even the human imagination.

# CHAPTER XIX

# RE-BIRTH

In the preceding chapter we have explained that the soul, falling into the second soul slumber, is caught up by the currents of the Karmic attraction, and is carried on toward re-birth in an environment, and with ties, in accordance with the sum of its character and desires. As we shall see in the succeeding chapter, some souls escape this current of rebirth, and are, instead, carried on to higher spheres of activity and being. But, by far, the great majority of the souls on the Astral Plane move forward toward earthly re-birth --- such being their Karma. But here, we must caution the student against falling into the far too common error of supposing that this Karma is a stern something meting out rewards and punishments according to some established code. Instead, Karma is simply the law of spiritual cause and effect --- we are punished not because of our sins, but by them we are rewarded not because of our good deeds, but by them. In short, our rewards and punishments arise by the very nature of our character, and our character is the sum total of our desires. Therefore, DESIRE is the motive power of Karma, and, through Karma, of our re-births.

To many, it seems as if re-birth upon earth is something forced upon the soul in spite of its desires. The very opposite is true, for the sum of the desires of the soul constitute the very actual motive power leading to the re-birth.

Those who are re-born on earth are not re-born against their will or desire. On the contrary, they are re-born because they actually desire it. They are carried into the current of re-birth because their tastes and desires have created longings that can be satisfied only by renewed life in the flesh. Although they are not conscious of it, they instinctively place themselves again within the operations of the Law of Attraction, and are swept on to re-birth, in exactly the environment best calculated to enable them to live out and outlive these desires --- to express and exhaust the force of desire. They hunger to satisfy their longings, and, until that hunger is appeased, the desires cannot be discarded. This does not mean that every desire must necessarily be lived out, for it happens frequently that new insight and experience causes the soul to turn with loathing from the former object of desire, and the desire thus dies a natural death. But so long as the desire remains alive it tends to attract the soul toward objects and environment which is likely to satisfy it. This is true of the soul on the Astral Plane, as well as in earth life.

Desire is always the great motive power of the soul in determining rebirth.

The soul, preserving its desire for material things --- the things of flesh and the material life --- and not being able to divorce itself from these things, will naturally fall into the current of re-birth which will lead it toward conditions in which these desires will flourish and , become manifest. It is only when the soul, by means of many earth-lives, begins to see the worthlessness and illusory nature of earthly desires, that it begins to become attracted by the things of the life of its higher nature, and, escaping the flowing currents of earthly re-birth, it rises above them and is carried to higher spheres. The average person, after years of earthly experience, is apt to say that he or she has no more desire for earth life, and that his or her only desire is to leave the same behind forever. These persons are perfectly sincere in their statements and beliefs, but a glance into their inmost soul would reveal an entirely different state of affairs. They are not, as a rule, really tired of earth-life, but merely of the particular kind of earth life which they have experienced during that incarnation. They have discovered the illusory nature of a certain set of earthly experiences, and feel disgusted at the same. But, they are still full of another set of desires, and of hunger for another set of experiences on earth. They have failed to find happiness or satisfaction in their own experience, but they will admit, if they are honest with themselves, that IF they could have had things "so and so," instead of "this and thus," they would have found happiness and satisfaction. The "if" may have been satisfied love, wealth, fame, gratified ambition, success of various kinds, etc. --- but, be it what it may, the "if "is nearly always there. and that "IF "really is the seed of their remaining desires. And the longing for that "if "is really the motive for the re-birth.

Very few persons would care to live over their earth life, according to their own statements --- and they are honest enough in the statement. But, like old Omar they would be perfectly willing to remake the world according to their heart's desire --- and then live the earth life. Do you see what we meant It is not earth life that is distasteful to them, but merely the particular experiences of earth-life which are disdained. Give to the average man and woman youth, health, wealth, talent, and love, and they will be very willing to begin the round of earth life afresh. It is only the absence of, or failure in, these or similar things, which causes them to feel that life is a failure --- a thing to be joyfully left behind.

The soul, in its sojourn on the Astral is rested, refreshed and reinvigorated.

It has forgotten the weariness of life which it had experienced during the previous incarnation. It is again young, hopeful, vigorous, and ambitious. It feels within itself the call to action --- the urge of unfulfilled desires, aspirations, and ambitions --- and it readily falls into the currents which lead it to the scene of action in which these desires may be manifested.

We have many instances of this change of feeling in earth-life. We feel tired, discouraged, nay, even disgusted, with our earthly affairs, at the close of the day, the year, or the exciting period. But rest, sleep, change of scene, and the influx of new impressions, make a change, and before long we are filled with longing for new activities and action. The majority of persons are not really tired of life, or disgusted with the things of life. They are merely experiencing the race impulse toward "something else, some other place "--- a change of scene and occupation would work a speedy cure for them. They are not world weary --- they are merely mentally and emotionally tired. And thus it is with the tired soul. Change its place of abode to the Astral, and give it the Elixir of Life --- and it is ready for another part to play in the Drama of Life.

Another point upon which there is much misunderstanding is the matter of the unconsciousness of the soul in the matter of choice of the environment of the new birth. It is true that in souls of low development, the process is almost wholly instinctive, and there is practically no conscious realization or choice in the matter. But when the soul begins to develop and unfold in spiritual knowledge, it begins to have spiritual insight and consciousness, and in many cases it sees dimly as in a dream, (during the second soul slumber) the conditions toward which it is being drawn, and often exercises a decided choice. In the case of a strong personality, provided the spiritual development is there, there is often more than a dreamlike choice, for such a soul does much to "make circumstances" for itself in its new birth, always within the limitations of its Karma, of course.

Another point, which should be cleared up, is that regarding the character of the desires which serve as the motive power for re-birth. It is not meant that these desires are necessarily low or unworthy desires or longings. On the contrary, they may be of the highest character, and might be more properly styled aspirations, ambitions, or high aims, but the principle of desire is in them all. Desires, high and low, are the seeds of action. And the impulse toward action is always the distinguishing feature of desire. Desire always wants to have things, or to do things, or to be things. Love, even of the most

81

unselfish kind, is a form of desire; so is aspiration of the noblest kind. A desire to benefit others is as much a desire as its opposite. In fact, many unselfish souls are drawn back into rebirth simply by the insistent aspirations to accomplish some great work for the race, or to serve others, or to fulfill some duty inspired by love. But, high or low, if these desires are connected in any way with the things of earth, they are re-birth motives and rudders.

But, in conclusion, let us say that no soul which does not in its inmost soul desire rebirth on earth will ever be so re-born. Such a soul is attracted toward other spheres, where the attractions of earth exist not. Its Karma carries it away from earth --- not toward it. But this is the condition of but few, although, little by little, every soul will experience it in the aeons to come. For all are on The Path, and spiritual evolution moves surely though slowly. Those who are interested in this higher life of the soul are invited to read the next, the last, chapter. If its words appeal to you, you have already taken the first steps toward the attainment.

# CHAPTER XX

## BEYOND REINCARNATION

Those who imagine that the Yogi Philosophy teaches that before the soul there is an endless chain of earthly re-births, or series of reincarnations, have failed to grasp the real spirit of the teaching. When it is remembered that the earth is but one of a countless number of preparatory worlds, having its beginning in time and its ending in time, the folly of such a doctrine becomes apparent. The earth is but one of the many schools, which have been from time to time formed in the Cosmos, and which, at the best, are but mere lower grade abodes. The soul of man will persist aeons after this earth, and millions of others like it, will have vanished into the ether of space from which it originally emerged. To assign to earth-life any such importance in the Cosmic order is contrary to the teachings of the wise.

Moreover, it is a false teaching which holds that even in the present era and phase of the soul's existence the soul can progress no further than earthly incarnation. Even though the majority of the race must undergo many earthly incarnations before freedom and liberation is found, still it is equally true that when a soul reaches the stage of spiritual development in which the ties of earth-life no longer bind it, then it is impossible that such a soul can be held to the round of earthly incarnation for even a moment of time.

There are many souls which are now on the Astral Plane, undergoing the final stages of the casting off of the earthly bonds. And there are many souls now in earth-life which will never again return to earth, but which, after their next sojourn on the Astral Plane, will rise to the higher planes of existence, leaving the earth and all earthly things behind forever. Moreover, there are to-day, on earth, thousands of souls which are well on the way to freedom, and which will have but one more earth-life to undergo --- and that one life will be passed in an exalted state of understanding and wisdom. At the present time we are nearing the end of a cycle in which a very great number of souls are preparing for their upward flight, and many who read these lines may be well advanced in that cyclic movement.

It would be the veriest folly for human pen to attempt to picture the nature of the existence on the higher spheres --- even those spheres only one grade higher than the earth. For there are no words which would convey the meaning --- no mental concepts which would embody the idea. Nay, more, the majority of the race have not even the mental machinery which would enable them to even think of the nature of such a life. The average human mind cannot begin to think even of the middle planes of the Astral, and the concept of the higher Astral is far beyond them. What then must be their position regarding the thought of realms of being to which even the highest Astral planes are but as dung-hills compared with the world's greatest palaces? Enough to know that there exists an infinite scale of being, composed of realm after realm, ever rising higher and higher and higher --- and that the soul is destined to move on and on and on toward the Infinite.

Escape from the round of earthly reincarnation is possible when the soul learns the truth regarding its own nature and its relation to the Whole. When it perceives the illusory nature of the phenomenal universe, and realizes that the spiritual world is the only real one, then do the ties of the material life begin to slip away, and the soul begins to struggle from its confining bonds. This liberation is the great end aimed at in the Yogi Philosophy. This is the reason, end, and aim, of Yoga. Some attain it by faithful works; others by love of the divine and of the divine fragment in their fellow human beings; others by the use of the intellect and the attainment of wisdom; others by development of the intuitive faculties; but all these are but different roads leading to the same end. When the nature of earthly things is realized, they lose their hold upon the human soul. Desire then dies away, and the soul is liberated and attains spiritual freedom. Loosened from the attraction of earth, the soul takes higher flights, and soars to the higher regions of being.

The philosophies of the Orient are filled with this idea. Under various guises it appears. To the initiated occultist the sacred teachings of the world --- of all religions --- are seen to have their esoteric side. And the spirit of the esoteric teaching is always Liberation. As we write these words, our eyes fall upon a book lying on our table --- a little story of the East, told by a Western writer. This writer has caught the spirit of the East and expresses it well. Listen to his words, and see how true they are to the spirit of the teaching:

"The object of the Sage, according to the old Hindoo doctrine, is to become absolute master of himself (jitama), to render himself completely superior, or rather indifferent to the 'attachment' of all mundane clogs. The ordinary mortal is a prisoner, tied, bound in bondage, or attached (sakta), to and by the objects of delusion and sense. Whoever aims at emancipation must first, by a long and strenuous course of penance and austerity, sever these attachments, till even though he still remains among them, they run off him like

84

water from a duck; and he goes on living, according to the classic formula, like a wheel that continues to revolve when the original impetus has ceased; or like a branch that goes on swaying after the departure of the bird. He is awake, as opposed to those who still remain blinded by illusion; he is free, as contrasted with the bound."

The above writer, however, has erred when he speaks of the "long and strenuous course of penance and austerity," necessary to sever the material attachments. The best authorities frown upon these ascetic practices and austerities, and do not encourage them. The true practice is that of the attainment of wisdom, and the opening of the heart to the inflow of the Divine Wisdom which comes in the form of Intuition. It needs but to perceive the real nature of material things in order to lose desire for them; therefore Knowledge is the great Liberator. It is true that great unselfish love (Bhakti Yoga) will cause the scales to fall from the eyes of the soul; it is likewise true that faithful works and duty performed without hope of reward (Karma Yoga), will cause the eyes to see clearly but the greatest of all Yoga is Gnani Yoga, the Way of Wisdom.

To those who yearn for release, we recommend a careful study of the Yogi Philosophy, or any of the other great forms of the Wisdom-Religion, and the careful following of the Life of the Spirit which is common to all religions, rightly understood. We think that the best little guide on The Path in the English language, is that little manual "Light on the Path," which is founded on occult axioms current even in ancient Atlantis. In this valuable little manual are to be found "The Rules which are written on the Walls of the Hall of Learning," by the "Rulers of the Golden Gate." As a writer has said: "What Parsifal is to lovers of music, that 'Light on the Path' is to aspiring souls --- a never-ending source of inspiration and wonder." The following axioms, taken from its pages, give the keynote, when rightly understood --- the balance of the manual is but an explanation of the axioms:

1. Kill out ambition.
2. Kill out desire of life.
3. Kill out desire of comfort.
4. Kill out all sense of separateness.
5. Kill out desire for sensation.
6. Kill out the hunger for growth.
7. Desire only that which is within you.
8. Desire only that which is beyond you.

9. Desire only that which is unattainable.

10. Desire power ardently.

11. Desire peace fervently.

12. Desire possessions above all

13. Seek out the way.

14. Seek the way by retreating within

15. Seek the way by advancing boldly without.

16. Stand aside in the coming battle and though thou lightest, be not thou the warrior.

17. Look for the warrior, and let him fight in thee.

18. Take his orders for battle, and obey him.

19. Listen to the song of life.

20. Store in your memory the melody you hear.

21. Learn from it the lesson of harmony.

22. Regard earnestly all the life that surrounds you.

23. Learn to look intelligently into the hearts of men.

24. Regard most earnestly your own heart.

25. Inquire of the earth, the air, and the water, of the secrets they hold for you.

26. Inquire of the holy ones of the earth, of the secrets they hold for you.

27. Inquire of the inmost, the one, of its final secret, which it holds for you throughout the ages.

28. Hold fast to that which has neither substance nor existence.

29. Listen only to the voice which is soundless.

30. Look only on that which is invisible alike to the inner and the outer sense."

These axioms have seven several and distinct meanings, superimposed one upon the other, and which are uncovered only by the unveiling of the eyes of the soul as it unfolds. Blessed is he who is able to comprehend even the first set of meanings, for he is on The Way.

The commentor upon these axioms, in the little manual, gives the following valuable advice to those who seek out the Way of Liberation and Peace:

"Seek in the heart the source of evil, and expunge it. It lives fruitfully in the heart of the devoted disciple, as well as in the heart of the man of desire. Only the strong can kill it out. The weak must wait for its growth, its fruition, its death. And it is a plant that lives and increases throughout the ages. It flowers when the man has accumulated unto himself innumerable existences. He who will enter upon the path of power must tear this thing out of his heart. And then the heart will bleed, and the whole life of the man seem to be utterly dissolved. This ordeal must be endured: it may come at the first step of the perilous ladder which leads to the path of life: it may not come until the last. But, 0 disciple, remember that it has to be endured, and fasten the energies of your soul upon the task. <u>Live neither in the present nor the future</u>, but in the eternal. This giant weed cannot flower there: this blot upon existence is wiped out by the very atmosphere of eternal thought."

The same commentor utters the following additional advice:

"Look for the flower to bloom in the silence that follows the storm not till then. It shall grow, it will shoot up, it will make branches and leaves and form buds, while the storm continues, while the battle lasts. But not till the harassed spirit. And in the deep silence, and melted --- not until it is held by the divine fragment which has created it, as a mere subject for grave experiment and experience --- not until the whole nature has yielded, and become subject unto its higher self, can the bloom open. Then will come a calm such as comes in a tropical country after a heavy rain, when Nature works so swiftly that one may see her action. Such a calm will come to the mysterious even will occur which will the whole personality of the man is dissolved prove that the way has been found. Call it by what name you will it is a voice that speaks where there is none to speak it is a messenger that comes, --- a messenger without form of substance, --- or it is the flower of the soul that has opened. It cannot be described by any metaphor. But it can be felt after, looked for, and desired, even amid the raging of the storm. The silence may last a moment of time, or it may last a thousand years, but it will end. Yet you will carry its strength with you. Again and again the battle must be fought and won. It is only for an interval that nature can be still."

In conclusion, let us again quote from the writer of the words above quoted --- words also inspired by a higher source of authority and wisdom:

### "The Three Truths"

"There are three truths which are absolute, and which cannot be lost, but yet may remain silent for lack of speech: (I) The soul of man is immortal, and its future is the future of a thing whose growth and splendor have no limit. (II) The principle which gives life dwells in us, and without us, is undying and eternally beneficent, is not heard or seen or felt, but is perceived by the man who desires perception. (III) Each man is his own absolute law-giver, the dispenser of glory or gloom to himself, the decreer of his life, his reward, his punishment. These truths, which are as great as is life itself, are as simple as the simplest mind of man. Feed the hungry with them."

And now, friend and reader, we leave you once more. We trust that what we have said will prove to be as the seeds of future trees of knowledge with in you. For this is the most that the teacher may hope to do--to plant seeds. We trust that have at least brought you to the doors of the perception of the truth that there is no Death---that what we call Death is but "the other side" of life, and one with it. May you may your own spiritual eyes become opened, that your may perceive these truths for yourself, and through your own experience. And now, once more, good student, we say to thee.

## PEACE UNTO OTHERS!

Made in the USA
Monee, IL
26 April 2022